Concubines and Bondservants

A Social History

Maria Jaschok

Zed Books Ltd.
London and New Jersey

Concubines and Bondservants: A Social History was first
published in 1988 by:

East Asia
Oxford University Press
Warwick House
Hong Kong

Rest of the World
Zed Books Ltd.
57 Caledonian Road
London N1 9BU

British Cataloguing in Publication Data
Jaschok, Maria
Concubines and Bondservants : a social history.
1. China. Women. Social conditions, to 1923
I. Title
350.4′ 2′0951
ISBN 0-86232-782-2
ISBN 0-86232-783-0 pbk

East Asia ISBN 0 19 584952 3

Library of Congress Cataloging-in-Publication Data

Jaschok, Maria.
Concubines and bondservants/Maria Jaschok.
p.   cm.
Bibliography: p.
ISBN 0–86232–782–2.   ISBN 0–86232–783–0 (pbk.)
1. Prostitution—China—History.   2. Concubinage—China—History.
3. China—Social life and customs.   4. China—Rural conditions.
I. Title.
HQ281.J37 1989
306.7′42′0951—dc19

Contents

Threads: Introduction

It was in Hong Kong, in 1978, that the first threads became visible. I had emerged from the airplane not knowing what to expect and what to be prepared for: I was overwhelmed by heat, the sheer unbearable noise of Hong Kong traffic, dizzying movements, and people, people . . .

My sense of alienation was depressing and acute; the sole purpose for coming to Hong Kong was the study of people with whom in this teeming city there seemed to be no possible point of contact and communication. In this early period of painful acclimatization my theoretical preparations in London seemed disturbingly irrelevant. What was relevant was the bewildering direct encounter with the Chinese population which my status as a European in a colonial set-up defined for me; without my volition I became drawn into relationships which based themselves on mystical beliefs in innate superiority and inferiority. Yet, with growing intimacy with Hong Kong society, what at a first superficial impression seemed a case of European arrogance and Chinese subservience turned out to be a much more complex multi-layered panorama of cross-ethnical resentment, racial chauvinism, mutual dislike and misunderstanding; or, at best, a stoical indifference.

While my archival work went on as planned, the search for Chinese contacts was slow and involved for me a sometimes painful exposure of myself. Painful because years of study confined to libraries are a poor preparation for personal commitment, involving the whole of the researcher's personality.

Already before I arrived in Hong Kong I knew that the *mooi-jai* problem could not be studied quantitatively.[1] I could only proceed on the assumption that among the older women of Hong Kong there were some who could tell their personal experiences: what it was like to be sold by their families into the urban families of Hong Kong and there to be used and worked as the owner saw fit; the age of the youngest survivors might be somewhere between 55 and 60.

But how was I to approach these women when family pride and sensitivity towards everything which could imply a loss of 'face' was more likely to induce their withdrawal from me? I had not even begun to approach the prior problem: how would I identify particular women as former mooi-jai? (Unlike the plantation-slaves of America their skin-colour in no way differed from that of their masters.) Here neither official contacts nor academic support could help – on the contrary, they might have hindered. This purgatorial time of enforced idleness ended only when suddenly my letter in a local daily paper and a subsequent radio interview brought about a response that amply recompensed for those long and seemingly futile weeks.

Among the letters I received in response to mine was one that constituted the starting point for the most vital phase in my work: Helen Chan, a member of the Meng family, told me she was curious to meet and talk. It was this relationship which gradually brought into my vision women from different generations and different mental enclosures – women who had affected her deeply and whose family lives revealed parallels with her own. This relationship – as my understanding of Helen Chan increased – informed me of the complexity of the subject matter I was trying to investigate.

I stayed in Hong Kong for nine months: learning about the patient acquisition of knowledge and understanding, about the constantly shifting perceptions that informants brought to bear upon the histories they had to tell; histories that therefore seemed always in a flux, affected by contemporary needs for new interpretations. My interviews were formal, sometimes, and informal, most of the time: sitting around the dinner table, walking through an exhibition, wandering through streets and crowded markets, looking at vegetables and fruits, visiting temples, or just driving through Hong Kong. Snatches of conversation, remarks made off-hand lingered – made me contemplate, take notes, pick up the threads again in a later conversation, when the moment seemed right. Imperceptibly my position in relation to the informants and their families underwent a change, from that of an outsider whose interest in them was clearly defined by my status as a student of Chinese history, to a friend and confidante with emotional commitments to one party rather than to the other in a family quarrel.

I, myself, became drawn into the currents of hostility that divided members of families, and into currents of age-old resentment, often scarcely admitted, that made me constantly go back in time and become the indefatigable questioner who was exploring an interpretation that would neither betray their life-histories nor my responsibility as a historian.

The bitterness and strife in Helen Chan's family began with the concubine-grandmother Moot Xiao-li. She died a long time ago, but her spirit has yet to be buried. She lives on in her daughter, as a benevolent presence – and in her grand-daughter, as a malignant foe. Moot Xiao-li continues to divide the clan and fuel bitterness between the families of her husband's sons and daughters. There are those who will lower their voices with respect when they recall her, there are those who will purse their mouths as if to spit at the mention of her name.

I never met Moot Xiao-li in person, but I learnt not to underestimate her. Her descendants testify to the indomitable personality she brought to bear on life. Their histories, their perceptions of their family's past provided me with the clues for my interpretation.

Part 1.   Motifs

1. Moot Xiao-li

The Moot Family[1]

> Destitute families sell these girls to certain go-betweens that fatten them (allow me the use of this word) in order to present them or sell them in the market of vice. Thus some of them enter bordellos as apprentices and some of them even become concubines of rich Chinese. Many go through hells of misery, suffering and brutality. The misery consumes their lives until they fall into such disgusting fates that we Europeans find it difficult to understand how the Chinese government can tolerate it.[2]

One of the many Chinese in 19th century Heungshan, Guangdong Province (present-day Zhongshan), who decided to leave the home village in order to seek a livelihood was an unemployed labourer of the name of Moot. He arrived in Macau accompanied by his wife and children. They built a makeshift hut on the hilly outskirts of the city, and he began to hawk thread. This was neither a secure nor a lucrative occupation, but at first they could make ends meet. More children were born. How many, no one knows. But the hawker Moot was forced to look for ways to make some additional money. Heaven had punished him with many daughters, only one son had born so far. Fortunately for Moot, in Macau it was possible to find people prepared to give money for young girls.

Moot did not sell his daughter directly into 'the market of vice' but to a go-between whose business was to buy girls as mooi-jai, only to resell them later, at a high price, to customers in Macau and Hong Kong.

Transmutations

Options for making profit out of daughters were manifold, contradicting the common lament that a daughter implied inevitable loss, as she was to be married away and thus contribute her productive and reproductive powers to a family other than her natal one.

Mooi-jai[3] – such a name was given to the girl after she had been through the customary transaction that was widespread and known all over China (*bei-nü* and *ya-tou* constituted its equivalent in the mandarin-speaking regions of China). It was a custom that was often the last resort of the financially desperate, a custom justified by reference to the traditional philanthropy of the wealthy, a custom that gave rise to widespread trafficking in females; reviled and defended and the subject matter of private action and government legislation, this custom lasted well into the 20th century.

My definition is broader than the official one adopted at the time of the Anti-Mooi-jai campaign in the 1920s (see Appendix A) as the vicissitudes that could befall a mooi-jai were more complex than allowed for in a narrow exposition. The official definition given in a Hong Kong Census Report of 1921, referring to 'all young girls whose parents have assigned their rights of guardianship to other families for a monetary consideration, and whose labour is at the free disposal of the new guardian till the age for marriage' – seems scarcely relevant to the histories of the mooi-jai related here – whether she had been Moot Xiao-li or Ma Xin's mooi-jai.[4] It also understated the factor of power. The mooi-jai custom was rooted in the sale of the girl and thus all rights connected with ownership were transferred to the master by her parents, guardian, or owner.

Often exploited for domestic purposes, she could also be transferred into brothels of the large cities, sold for a number of years into contract labour, *bao-fan*, where the earnings of a contracted factory-worker ended up in the pockets of the contractor, or she could be trained by her owner for prostitution. Her servitude might be temporary; it could, however, also culminate in prolonged and at times indefinite states of slavery.

Upper- and middle-class families often kept a *jong-ga-mooi*, a girl who comprised part of a bride's marriage dowry. The jong-ga-mooi shared with the mooi-jai the features of sale and unconditional ownership; both could become 'the other' when resold or presented as a gift. Thus the mooi-jai might be disposed of by her owner as a present for the bride, and then might find herself performing the work of a jong-ga-mooi, that is, instead of personal assistance to her mistress be responsible for the more general, and physically more exhausting work in the household.

The mooi-jai might also turn into a *cho-jue-fa* and the owner would realize a handsome profit with her sale into prostitution. Some critics of this practice declared the mooi-jai custom to be the greatest feeder of the brothel.[5]

Daughters of rich men, when they celebrated their sixth birthday, often received as a present a nine-year old mooi, a *luk-gau-mooi*, who, according to the ancient custom, was to bring luck to the young mistress. This mooi accompanied the young mistress and served her personally, often for a lifetime.

The *tung-yeung sik*, or little daughter-in-law, was equally a consequence of poverty. Intended to save poor families the expenses involved in taking a more mature bride for their sons, abuses of this custom led to the girl being used as a life-long servant instead of being married when of suitable age.[6]

CHART 1
The Moot family

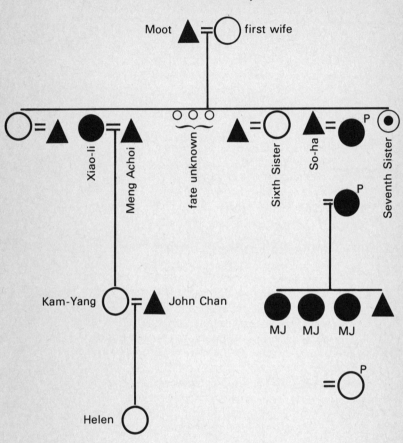

 male

◯ female   MJ   mooi-jai

= married   P   prostitute

⬤ sold   ⊙   died before
                        marriage

The Moot Family

Xiao-li's mother had always been weak physically, and the frequent pregnancies weakened her further, so her second daughter – at that time six or seven years old (it is believed she was born in 1882) – already performed most household tasks, together with her eldest sister. But she still found time to roam around the hill, unsupervised, and to assert herself as an independent spirit toughened by rivalries with other children who joined her games. This freedom was suddenly terminated.

Yip Min-yuk, by profession a *daai-kam-je*, a ritual specialist, who would be hired by families for the duration of the wedding to attend to the bride, may have been known personally to Moot, or may have been mentioned to him as a suitable go-between – anyway, at some point he approached her. He was poor, and unlucky in having too many daughters; Yip Min-yuk offered her services.

Xiao-li was not consulted about the sale, naturally. Moot was known as a strong-headed man and the prospect of handy cash must have been a powerful counterweight to any feeling of remorse about losing his daughter, so his great-grand-daughter told me. Poverty left him no choice, his grand-daughter interpreted for me. Before the amah left for Guangzhou, Xiao-li had changed hands. The sale was unconditional and the amah reserved the right to decide the girl's future as she saw fit. It seems that the girl was simply told to put her few belongings into a bundle and to accept the parting from her family and friends. What pain she felt, or what excitement, about impending changes is difficult to imagine. The fact that it was not uncommon in Macau at that time to sell a daughter may make this appear 'just another case' in a familiar pattern; but, unlike a historian, Xiao-li knew only it happened to *her*, and that she had to leave whatever she had learned to love and cherish during her seven years. That Xiao-li was attached to her family she showed later when, as a wealthy concubine, she sought out her natal family to give them some of her riches. As a rich woman she could easily have ignored her father's existence, but the force of filial obligation, even under these circumstances, proved stronger than any judgement on his decision to sell her.

It is said that the money her father received for Xiao-li enabled him to stop hawking and to devote himself to gambling. He never worked again; when short of money, he sent his children to collect leftover food from hotel and restaurant kitchens. After the reunion with his daughter she provided him with a regular income, enough to make him and his son two of the most notorious members of the Chinese gambling circuit in Macau.

The Daai-kam-je, Yip Min-yuk

Buyers of mooi-jai could come from any social stratum, could purchase a girl on behalf of an organized gang specializing in the trafficking of women,

CHART 2

Yip Min-Yuk's establishment in Guangzhou

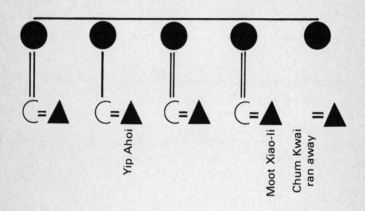

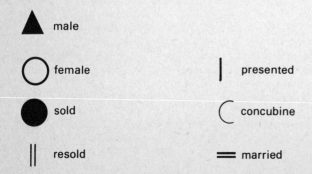

male

female

sold

resold

presented

concubine

married

or buy girls for personal use.

Of interest is a category of single women, to which Yip Min-yuk belonged. Within this category were Daoist nuns who often would purchase a mooi-jai to adopt as a foster-daughter and carry on their name and profession. Boat-women might buy little girls to help them with their trade and support them in old age. Prostitutes and brothel-keepers bought them to enter the profession of a prostitute; sometimes they were used to work in the brothel, sometimes sold as concubines. Daai-kam-je and amahs (domestic servants) were known to buy girls whom they did not keep for their own use, or whom they might train for a number of years and then sell to the highest bidder. A Chinese witness in Hong Kong told an official investigation into the mooi-jai practice, carried out in 1936, that 'a class, usually high class servants, buy them [girls] young and when they retire sell them as concubines or prostitutes'.[7]

In the capacity of a daai-kam-je, Yip Min-yuk had unique access to the inner rooms of high class and rich families – being able to utilize from this excellent vantage point observations and gossip for her own ends. As an attendant to the central person in the household, the would-be bride, she was accessible to father, brother, or uncle of the bride, who might want to avail themselves of her service. She could use the opportunity to assess the taste and preferences of a potential mooi-jai buyer and the degree of effort needed to sway the household women into supporting a new acquisition. Yip Min-yuk had customers among many of the wealthy and respectable Chinese in Guangzhou, Hong Kong, and Macau. According to Xiao-li's daughter, Yip was well-known and popular, attending invariably 'on the high and mighty'.

Yip was a successful businesswoman of some economic independence and she conducted her not unprofitable sideline of raising and selling young girls at her own establishment in Guangzhou. When Xiao-li entered the establishment, in the late 1880s, she joined three other mooi-jai and one so-called 'vestal virgin' (that was how my informant referred to the girl who was one day to worship at the daai-kam-je's family altar after her death). The mooi-jai assisted Yip Min-yuk in her capacity as a daai-kam-je; they also performed household duties, and spent the rest of the time learning the rudiments of a courtesan's skills. Yip Min-yuk knew she could increase her investment at least fourfold when reselling her mooi-jai.

As Chan Kam-yang told me, Yip Min-yuk was popular because she knew all 'the right classical phrases'. For example, she could tell the bride how properly to greet the bridegroom's attendants when leaving the bridal chair, how to greet the parents-in-law at the kow-tow ceremony. 'She was clever and shrewd and made a lot of money'.

For the record I must tell of Yip's end, which was related to me by Helen Chan, and prefaced with the words, 'the rightful retribution'.

Yip Min-yuk died from an overdose of opium in Macau; no sooner was she dead than her mooi-jai stripped the corpse of all valuables. Not trusting anyone, she had been used to carrying around receipts and papers on her body. When these were found, the bereaved went to Hong Kong on the assumption that the papers would entitle them to collect the rest of Yip's fortunes from a Hong Kong bank. But she had been banking with a former client who, when approached by these claimants, refused to hand over the money. As it emerged later, the fortune was handed over to Moot Xiao-li's daughter, with whom he stayed until her death in 1980.

Yip Min-yuk did not necessarily suffer moral opprobrium as a result of her activities. As an unattached woman she did well in economic terms; not only that, she supported her natal family and her unemployed brother (who is said to have had criminal connections) proving herself a filial daughter and devoted sister. Having, as a woman, fewer options for making money she exploited those which came within the traditional domain of female life: marriage, concubinage, and domesticity. Where the parties to a marital transaction were rich and socially well-respected she attended to the rituals and provided her knowledge of traditional rites. Observing the rite of passage from virginity to womanhood and a new status, she was also aware of the supreme importance implied in the exchange of bridal gifts and the mutual recognition of social ties and obligations.

In the households of wealthy urban Chinese families she observed the merging of tradition and new ways. Tradition still applied when a *daai-poh* (first wife) was chosen for the son of the house. Traditional were the rituals and the employment of fortune-tellers and go-betweens, as well as those of ritual specialists. The first wife was chosen as an asset, and considerations of her family's status were important for keeping face. But there were also new ways of behaviour; in the course of the 20th century women were often simply taken as mistresses, rather than chosen as concubines. Concubines, openly taken for sexual gratification, were purchased from the great market in human beings which flourished then in China and Hong Kong. The 'new ways' meant that concubines could also be more easily cast off, with a lump sum payment.

Yip knew of this demand (these were the kinds of households she attended) and transformed it into a commercial proposition. She may have seen her trade as a beneficial act towards the girls who, as poor outsiders, got the chance to join rich households and thus 'make their fortune'. But the mooi-jai owned by the daai-kam-je were bought, owned unconditionally, kinless and under their purchaser's control. In every sense of the word, they were slaves. To Yip Min-yuk they were girls bought from the poor (rewarded with a sum of cash) whom she would profitably sell to the rich. She was good at this and would see to it that the girls would not upset her plans. For the mooi-jai the only alternative was to run away, and that would have meant that as unprotected females in Guangzhou they would have been prey to fates uncertain and probably much worse than what the daai-kam-je held out to them. She saw herself as performing a necessary function in a society where profit could be made from what China possessed in plenty – unattached females.

What was it like to be owned by a woman who had invested in a mooi-jai? A simple and yet the most difficult question to answer when one was young in age and impressionable – but also old enough to have discovered the difference between being part of a kin group, and belonging to no one – to have experienced the difference between being ruled by paternal authority and by power acquired by virtue of a deed of sale.

What the girls' training was like no one has been able to tell me in detail. It appears, however, that manuals of sex techniques were used to prepare the mooi-jai for the day when they would be sold as concubines.[8] What must have been in the daai-kam-je's mind was the thought that wealthy and elderly (not to say old) men, who demanded special skills to achieve the satisfaction that inexperienced women could not provide, would pay highly for young virgins. At times these men were so decrepit that without the woman's active contribution little result could be achieved. The girls were taught sex techniques, but not the refinements achieved by some high-class prostitutes who, in the process of training for their profession, were often able to educate themselves.

Household tasks allocated to the mooi-jai were not heavy, because this would have meant spoiling the goods. The relationships formed among the girls were partly competitive, partly sisterly. They taught each other to smoke tobacco, and the daai-kam-je, herself an ardent opium smoker, turned a blind eye to this habit. The girls would remain in touch with each other after they had been sold. Helen Chan told me that they never forgot (not that they talked about it) that they 'came from the same walk of life'.

Something of the histories of the other mooi-jai and their subsequent lives was related to me (see Chart 2). The first mooi-jai became the sixth concubine to a rich old man. The third and fourth, too, brought good profit as concubines to aged men who could afford to keep several wives and mistresses. The second mooi-jai, reputed to have been the best looking, was given to Yip Ahon, who may have been Yip Min-yuk's favourite brother, or (it was claimed this was the more likely reason) she may have been under pressure to do him a favour, as family members were commonly in the same business. Yip Ahon was a member of a secret society in Guangzhou and it was said that from time to time Yip Min-yuk had to pay him protection money – in cash and kind. As is illustrated by Xiao-li's relationship with her younger brother when she was a rich concubine, wherever human trafficking went on, gangsterism was never far away.

The fifth mooi-jai, Chum Kwai, was (to quote Helen Chan) kept 'for worship as a long-haired nun'. It was intended that this girl stay at the daai-kam-je's home and worship at her ancestral tablets. She was to remain celibate and dedicate herself entirely to prayer. But, so the story goes, when the daai-kam-je was away on business, a married neighbour managed to get into her house and persuaded the young novice to part with her virginity, a handsome sum of money from Yip Min-yuk's savings, and to throw in her lot with him; one year later Chum Kwai gave birth to twins. Helen Chan could never tell me this well-known anecdote without breaking into a prolonged chuckle. To her, Chum Kwai's story had an important symbolic significance, namely, that women could break out from external constraints and 'get away'. Chan Kam-yang, Helen's mother, reacted quite differently. She had known Yip Min-yuk well and referred to her adamantly and demonstratively as 'my mother's foster mother'.

Xiao-li made a success of her opportunities as concubine, as Yip Min-yuk continued to stay in touch with her former mooi-jai. When Chan Kam-yang was a few years old Yip commented on her attractions, 'even her bottom can make music'. Chan Kam-yang told me this as a great compliment to herself and to the judgement of the daai-kam-je! But her daughter was disgusted and exclaimed at the vulgarity of 'that woman' and her preoccupations.

As I pointed out earlier, it was not uncommon for unmarried Chinese women of Yip Min-yuk's status to adopt girls to provide for them in old age and as insurance against potential financial calamities. The practice of raising young girls in Buddhist nunneries to ensure succession and economic security is still customary in present day Hong Kong.[9]

Yip Min-yuk had lost out on Chum Kwai, a most reluctant virgin. But this loss was offset by the profit she made on the other mooi-jai whom she had sold to the highest bidder, irrespective of the conditions and circumstances in which these women had to spend their future lives. This type of transaction gave rise to the comment by a critical observer of the mooi-jai institution that:

> The selling of young girls as concubines for mere profit is one of the evils that arises from the transference of infants and girl children for valuable consideration, and from this it is right and reasonable to protect them.[10]

When Xiao-li was about 15 years old Yip was called to attend on a bride of the rich Meng family in Hong Kong. She took Xiao-li with her, and she was thus introduced to her future family. The head of the household was Meng Achoi, an ailing comprador in his seventies, who required a concubine – Xiao-li was chosen.

Chen Dong-yuan describes the age-old ritual of selecting a young girl for concubinage (*shou-ma*) as follows:

> There are scores of people in Yangzhou who make their living out of shou ma. Those who wish to buy a concubine must not let their intentions be known, for as soon as the news gets around, procuresses and brokers gather round the buyer's gate like flies attracted by smell, who will not go away however much one chases them off. At dawn they clamour for the door to be opened. The go-between who arrived first brings the buyer out; the others follow closely behind, to await their turn.
>
> When they arrive at the [shou ma's] house, they sit down and drink tea, and the procuress leads in a [shou ma] saying, "Pay your respects to

the guests" and the girl does so. Then she commands "Walk forward" – "Turn around" – so the girl turns around to face the light, and thus to show her face. Then the woman asks "Let us see your hands" so the girl pushes up her sleeves to reveal her hands, arms and her skin. At the command "Look at the guest" she glances sidelong at him, thus showing her eyes. Then she is asked "How old are you" and she gives her reply, so the customer can hear her voice. The procuress says "Walk around again", and pulls back the girl's skirt to reveal her feet.

... Then the girl is told to come back. As one girl leaves the room, another enters; in each house there are about five or six girls to see, all follow the same procedure. If the buyer chooses a girl, he places a golden hairpin or jewel in her hair – this is called *cha dai*. Those who have not chosen anyone take out a sum of money to give to the procuress, or to a servant of the house. Then he goes elsewhere to carry on looking.

If the procuress tires, then there are plenty of others eager to take their turn. The proceedings may continue for one, two or even five days, if she does not tire of it. So, the customer may see as many as fifty to sixty girls.[11]

Chan Kam-yang supplemented this account for me. For connoisseurs of young girls particular emphasis was placed on compatible odour. Even the most attractive face could not compensate for odour which displeased the client. After having inspected teeth and breath, the girl was made to raise her arms, so that the odour of her armpits could be determined. To establish the vital vaginal odour, a date was sometimes inserted into the vagina of the girl inspected and then handed to the client. Some clients, not satisfied with smelling the date, might lick the fruit.

Xiao-li satisfied the buyer. The price paid for her is not known, but is said to have been several times the amount that Yip Min-yuk had paid for her.

Whether at that time Meng's first wife (daai poh) was dying or had only recently joined her ancestors is a point still hotly debated among members of the Meng lineage. But most informants agree that Meng took a concubine during the stipulated one year of mourning by a husband for his wife. Meng Achoi's indifference to the conventional mourning obligations was derived not only from perfunctory conjugal relations, but also illustrated a characteristic use of expediency when it came to tradition.[12] By taking a concubine, Meng Achoi sacrificed even the outward pretensions of a Confucianist gentleman.

The Comprador Meng Achoi

Meng Achoi was a member of the small prominent Chinese élite whose influence and fortune constitute an integral part of Hong Kong's history.

By the time the Colony had been formally established and its government granted the Royal Charter in 1843, the administration found itself faced with a rapidly growing Chinese population – seeking work and stability, and fleeing from insecure political conditions, unrelieved poverty, and an oppressive social system in their homeland.[13] These early settlers' humble background shaped the British administrators' perceptions of those administered as being composed exclusively of persons of 'low character'. Only in the 1860s, with the formation of a Chinese élite in Hong Kong, did these perceptions come to be challenged. And yet, the early Chinese élite shared the humble background of their less successful compatriots.

Generally speaking, the missionary school had provided the most important means of advancement for the typical member of the élite. In fact, the Christian Church – by providing educational opportunities, and the all-important English language instruction, for those who otherwise, by reason of birth and lack of options at home, would have had no access to education – was a positive, if inadvertent, agent in the creation of the Chinese financial élite.[14]

Arguably, compradors and merchants[15] were the two most important groups within the Chinese élite. In the social history of China compradors constituted a new amorphous grouping. Neither gentry nor traditional merchants: nevertheless, in the context of the 19th century treaty-ports they acquired the status and influence of the gentry and the economic power of the merchants to constitute a kind of 'commercial gentry'. Moulded by the Chinese traditional culture they were, however, not bound by it; although participants in Western technological developments, they yet responded selectively.[16]

In Hong Kong, the development of the comprador system accelerated with the outbreak of the Second Sino-British War in 1856, when foreign firms sought refuge from disturbed conditions in Guangzhou. Hong Kong in the 1850s and 1860s was the time of the great compradors; vast fortunes were made by their capital investments in commercial, financial, and industrial enterprises.[17]

For many compradors, employment with one firm was only a stepping-stone towards more lucrative business alone or in a syndicate with others. Their careers were often variations on the 'rags to riches' story. The comprador of the P&O Steamship Company, Kwok Acheong, though born in humble circumstances, was, when he died in 1880, the third biggest rate payer in Hong Kong, and worth nearly half a million dollars.[18]

The case of the successful merchant A-quei (or A-kwei) received publicity, in somewhat disapproving tone, from the Reverend George Smith:

> He possessed about fifty houses in the bazaar, and lived on the rent, in a style much above the generality of Chinese settlers, who are commonly composed of the refuse of the population of the neighbouring mainland. During the war, A-quei acted as purveyor of provisions to the British armament, and acquired some wealth. After the peace, he was at first

afraid to return to the mainland, lest he should be seized as a traitor by the Mandarins. In the end he settled at Hong Kong, where he is said to encourage disreputable elements by the loan of money, and in various ways to reap the proceeds of profligacy and crime.[19]

The marginal social origins of these élite members engendered weakened commitment to Confucian private and social values, and an easier embrace of Western commercial practices. But while their public face expressed their role as 'bicultural middlemen between East and West', material success also generated a desire to use traditional means to impress this success on members of their own culture. The tension generated by conflicting psychological and social demands, derived from a deeply conservative self-image and a commercially competitive environment, became manifest in the life-style of the typical élite member.

Three institutions had been created in 19th century Hong Kong that were:

to crystallize the relationships between a series of associations and to make plain the hierarchization and ranking of these associations; in other words, to provide a guide to the steps by which a Chinese acquired status in colonial Hong Kong.

This 'triumvirate of permanent boards and committees' consisted of the District Watchmen Committee (1866) which was the oldest and most influential of the three; the Tung Wah Committee (1870); and the Po Leung Kuk (1878).[20]

As J. Lethbridge suggested, many prominent Chinese were thus given the opportunity to express their support for British rule, were provided with an official and political role in Hong Kong society and an institutionalized validation of their acquired status.

Membership of the committees of the Po Leung Kuk and the Tung Wah and of the permanent committees of these two societies and the District Watch (a body of watchmen paid for by Chinese subscribers) helped meet this need. There was, thus, a relationship historically and sociologically between a growth in the numbers of prominent (i.e. rich and influential) Chinese and a growth in prestigious voluntary associations and official Chinese committees.[21]

Membership of this triumvirate could, in turn, pave the way for the most coveted of all memberships, that of the Legislative Council. These Chinese became truly 'the bedrock of local order and prosperity, and were recognized as such by the more perceptive British administrators.'[22]

Meng Achoi's life and career reveal many parallels with the life of the typical élite member. He was born, some time in the late 1820s, in the Heungshan, now Zhongshan district, in Guangdong province.[23] At some unknown stage in life he received sufficient training in the English language to distinguish him from most of his Chinese contemporaries.[24] It is known that he spent his youth in Rangoon, Burma, his humble background and poor expectations having driven him to seek his fortune outside native boundaries. The disassociation from familial roots certainly facilitated his later assimilation into a small group of Chinese who were dependent for their privileges on a colonial administration. Starting out as a clerk in the early 1850s Meng Achoi became a comprador with an American firm when it was removed from Guangzhou to Hong Kong, around 1858, at the time of the second Sino-British war.[25]

Previously he had been active as an interpreter, thus occupying all the 'typical' posts then open to Chinese with a Western-language background. He later took on other compradorships, as was common, and during the 1880s and 1890s he acted as a comprador for another American firm in Hong Kong.

Meng had turned the substantial rewards accessible to members of his privileged circle to good use. On 8 December 1858, he purchased his first piece of property and over the years continued to invest in property until he became one of the largest real-estate owners in Hong Kong, buying either as an individual or as a member of a syndicate.[26] In 1872, a new period of depression commenced, culminating in the collapse of the American firm with which Meng had his main dealings as a comprador. This collapse seemed to have curtailed his commercial activities. With the exception of his employment with Schellhaus & Co., during the 1880s and 1890s, I could discover no other evidence that he had been employed by other firms.

The events in 1872, however, seem not to have diminished his public status; in 1883 he was appointed a Justice of the Peace,[27] a highly prestigious post that he seems to have held until at least 1900, after which there is no mention of him.[28]

As I have already pointed out, typical social indicators for public status and prestige were: membership of important committees or boards supervising charitable institutions; publicized charitable contributions; attendance at government and social functions; and participation in important petitions and the like. A compilation of such a list for Meng Achoi provides tentative evidence that although he must be accounted a member of the small class of rich Chinese, it is by no means clear that he belonged to the inner core of this group.[29] Unaccountable absences from what must have been important prestigious functions, from widely-publicized subscription lists, and so on, could well point to his rank as being relatively inferior to the prime élite. Inconclusive data must make this a qualified statement, but it would, to some extent, explain the lack of biographical data on a successful Chinese entrepreneur, in contrast to certain contemporaries about whom an abundance of information is available. But even with these reservations, there is no doubt that Meng must have counted as one of the wealthier and more successful Chinese in Hong Kong. He was, for example, one of the first Chinese to live in the

CHART 3

The Household of Meng Achoi in the late 1890s

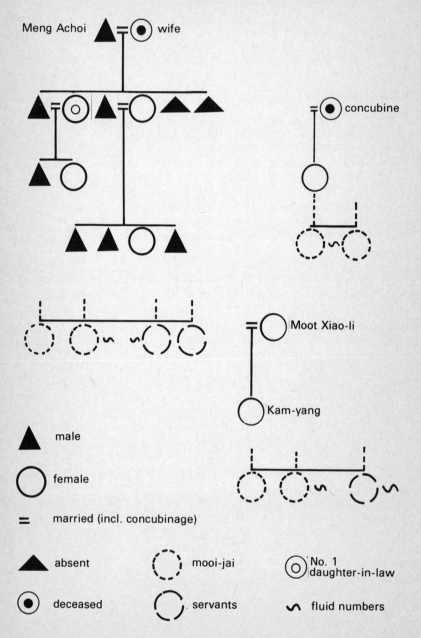

hitherto European-reserved 'mid-levels' in Hong Kong.

This outline of Meng's career, from humble beginnings to a wealthy and privileged position in Hong Kong, was not untypical for men from his social stratum. Having in their youth dissociated themselves physically and mentally from the strictures of Confucianist society – which would have kept them 'in their place' – in a colonial context they were able to exploit the demand for mediators between the West and the East to build up careers of social distinction and economic fortune.

Moot Xiao-li: Insiders and Outsiders

When, in the late 1890s, Xiao-li became Meng Achoi's concubine, the green-curtained sedan chair carried her to a family in which power and authority had passed into the hands of persons who envisaged no challenge to them. Meng Achoi seemed only a figure-head; old and ailing, severe bouts of gout had nearly paralysed him. The task of nursing had fallen on the shoulders of the first daughter-in-law who managed the household and its finances; as Meng Achoi's first wife and his previous concubine were dead, the domestic responsibilities were entirely in her hands. At that time, to hire a professional nurse was not common and the need to care for the old man was irksome to the first daughter-in-law. Thus she had conceived of the idea to fulfil the old man's whims (he wanted a young concubine) and to get a nurse for him in the bargain. When the daai-kam-je, Yip Min-yuk, introduced her mooi-jai Xiao-li, the bargain was struck to the satisfaction of all transacting parties.

Meng's townhouse, situated in a respectable and prestigious part of Hong Kong, was one of a total complex of four houses, all owned by Meng Achoi. Two had been rented out, the other two, which were connected, were occupied by the Meng family. They were demolished in the 1950s and no trace remains; I was not, therefore, able to obtain photographs of them and had to rely for a description on the selective memory of Chan Kam-yang, who had lived there as a child and young woman (until her 30th year), and on Helen Chan, who, all her childhood, had listened to stories about life in that house, told to her by her mother and by the first wife's grandchildren, who had shared the premises but not the concubine's life-style.

Entering from the street through the front door, one arrived in the general living area on the ground floor, where the dining-room was situated. A sliding door opened up to a large and spacious sitting room which, in turn, invited one for a leisurely walk out to a shady terrace overlooking a beautifully kept lawn and flower-bed. From the ground floor hall, stairs led up to a corridor on the first floor from which all the upstairs rooms could be reached; sliding doors connected these to each other. Meng Achoi occupied half of the house and there Xiao-li joined him to live as his concubine. The other half had been allocated to Meng's second son and

CHART 4

Private realm – the Meng household

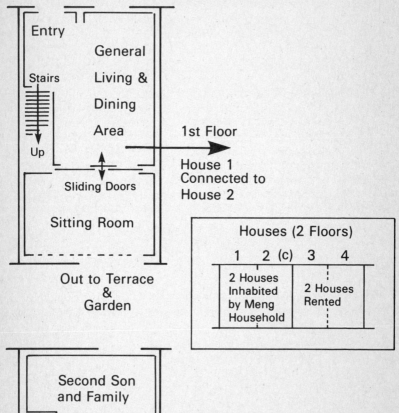

Street

Entry

General Living & Dining Area

Stairs

Up

1st Floor

House 1 Connected to House 2

Sliding Doors

Sitting Room

Out to Terrace & Garden

Houses (2 Floors)

1   2 (c)   3   4

2 Houses Inhabited by Meng Household

2 Houses Rented

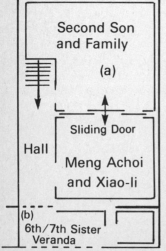

Second Son and Family

(a)

2nd Floor

Sliding Door

Hall

Meng Achoi and Xiao-li

(b)
6th/7th Sister
Veranda

(a) the close proximity to Meng Achoi's room made the women in the second son's family carriers of gossip about Xiao-li's life-style

(b) Xiao-li had invited her 6th sister, later her 7th sister, to stay with her, thus arousing hostility among the Meng women who resented another unwelcome addition to the household

(c) the second house was inhabited by the powerful first daughter-in-law and her family

family. But only Meng Achoi's half in the front opened up to a large verandah, on the one side of which the toilet had been built. The second house was constructed along the same lines and provided a home for the rest of the Meng family.

The two houses formed a mutually interdependent unit, with the first daughter-in-law as the undisputed mistress. She controlled the purse-strings, managed the expenditures and servants' pay, and ruled as autocratically over the family as she did over the numerous servants, whose quarters were in the basements of the two houses. Each family had servants, and each of the women their personal mooi-jai. Although every morning the head of the household, supported by his servants, made his domestic tour of inspection, he had handed over the active management to the strong woman who was his first son's wife.

This son had been a disappointment to Meng Achoi; he failed to emulate his father's successful career and instead remained a clerk, never achieving the distinction of becoming a comprador. Born to the first wife, in 1861, by the time he entered public life, the status of clerks had become less prestigious than it had been for the first generation of Chinese in Hong Kong. Meng's other sons shared the eldest's weak and ineffectual personality; one son had to disappear suddenly from Hong Kong because of charges that he had swindled his firm out of considerable sums of money.

Compradors of a certain standing commonly gave their sons a Western education, mostly abroad, which would afford them a distinct advantage for careers in Hong Kong as solicitors, lawyers, doctors – the 'in' professions for ambitious young Chinese. The sons of Meng Achoi had received sufficient schooling and English language education, but compared to the sons of similarly placed compradors their educational achievements were substandard. This anomaly may have been a reflection on their intelligence or motivation, or it may have indicated a decline in Meng's fortunes after his firm's collapse.

None of Meng's sons displayed strength and breadth of character. The second son, according to his daughter, was a devoted father and husband, the only son who took neither concubines nor mistresses, but in his working life as a clerk he was a crook and swindler 'who was even inept at swindling'.[30] Two of Meng's other sons left their families to live on the mainland with concubines. All of them were weak and dependent, totally submissive to the father, smothered emotionally by mothers and numerous servants. The authority of these men was precarious, yet they continued to be propped up – publicly – by structural paradigms of male dominance and superiority. Raised and indoctrinated with belief in their own infallibility, they were 'towers of male authority' only in so far as their female nurturers continued to provide the props. Having learnt to perceive themselves as masters of the universe, they came to depend on their dependants for the perpetuation of the sexual status quo. When Meng Achoi called his sons before him he expected them to kneel in front of him, showing his displeasure by bombarding them with handy objects. These scenes of humiliation with their father were obliterated when their wives and servants could be made to tremble under the masters' anger.

The boundaries of the women's territory were set not so much by men as individual actors, but by the rules of patriarchal society that both men and women had to respect as a thing apart from the strength or weakness of the *individual* male. Within these boundaries, on the 'inside', women faced women as rivals: for emotional hold over 'key' males; for financial control; for power over others.

The most important woman Xiao-li had to confront was the mistress of the house, the eldest son's wife. Here my informants, regardless of whether they were descended from the daai-poh (first wife) or the mooi-jai-cum-concubine, for once agreed: this woman had a pronounced streak of cruelty in her character. But she was also clever and capable and the saying went that even 'her toes were making money'. Proud of her superior background – she was the daughter of a high official in Guangzhou – no other woman in the household was allowed to forget this fact. She owned at least four mooi-jai, sometimes more, and was renowned for her harsh and indifferent treatment of them. Her most favoured punishment was to beat their fingers with the handle of a feather duster, after having tied them tightly over a chopstick. Like many upper-class women she spent much of her time gambling and as household duties took up her time during the day, she rested during the afternoon and got up in the evening to devote the better part of the night to playing mah-joong. She was a passionate player and since she did not like to be disturbed by having to play the hostess, the mooi-jai were expected to stay up to pour the tea and fan the players when the night was hot and humid. These mooi-jai had little sleep as they were expected to rise early the next morning to serve in the household. Lack of sleep made them drowsy and when their fanning ceased they were severely punished.

It was this woman who, when her son raped a mooi-jai, sold the girl to a brothel. It was customary for a mooi-jai to attend when the young masters of the house took a bath, ostensibly 'to keep the ghosts out of the bath-tub'.[31] The mooi-jai was supposed to stand with her back to the young master but at times he would take advantage of such opportunity and sexually assault the girl. What my informants criticized was not only the fact that the pregnant mooi-jai was sold, but that she was sold into one of the most notorious brothels in Guangzhou, low-class and frequented by rough coolies. According to an anecdote from that particular brothel, young virgins who had been kidnapped from the countryside, and who refused to be deflowered, were forced to submit in humiliating ways. A kitten was placed on their genitals and the trousers tightly belted. Then the kitten was tormented by beating its legs, causing it to claw at the girl's clitoris.[32]

The first daughter-in-law was arrogant, proud of her class and of her bound feet – the symbol of her class-membership – and confident of her power over the other women in the Meng household. These, although all from respectable families (all daai-poh had bound feet), had been brought up to obey and submit. Married to the younger sons of the house, their hierarchical standing was clearly defined and the dominance of the first daughter-in-law unquestioned. The various concubines of the sons had been brought in by the daai-poh as jong-ga-mooi (part of their dowry), and in subservience to their mistresses were even less likely to challenge the household's power structure. In every respect, Xiao-li, Meng Achoi's new concubine, was to obey the first daughter-in-law's rulings as blindly as did everyone else. Tradition, class, education, and the confident expectation that one day her son would be the head of the family, appeared to make her position invincible.

When Xiao-li entered the household she was young and it was the first time that she lived in such grandeur and style. While she was not long left in doubt of where the real influence lay, she herself was not lacking in resources. Unhindered by female models of passive acquiescence, toughened by material deprivation in her childhood and the need for survival against all odds, trained by a shrewd and worldly woman, who had exploited for her own ends in-built social prejudices against women, Xiao-li was no 'frog in the well', no lily-footed woman, but a calculating strategist who quickly realized where her source of power and strength would lie and how to utilize it.

Something happened that no one in the family Meng had foreseen. The old man, feeble in body and advanced in age, succumbed to the charms and attractions of the young woman. Nothing was good enough for her; Xiao-li craved all the things she associated with a life of luxury – and she got them. Delicacies were bought to satisfy her appetite for the exotic, pet animals were ordered to indulge her. The old man, already half-senile, was seeking immortality. Upsetting traditional tenets of ancestral worship, not his descendants, but the concubine, constituted the old man's lifeline, his link with a past virility and the promise of a future, however illusory. He desired not worship by descendants, but the worship of a young, attractive woman who flattered him with a fleeting sensation of youth and timelessness. The first daughter-in-law had underestimated the extent to which Xiao-li, young and pretty, would be able to utilize the relationship with the head of the family. 'My grandmother was the most successful sex-object', commented her grand-daughter.

Until the new concubine moved into Meng Achoi's room, it had been customary for the whole family to share the main meals. This custom ceased soon after Xiao-li's arrival. She and Meng Achoi took their meals in their room and it quickly became known that better food was served there, while the rest of the household continued to eat their usual fare. The concubine was slowly freeing herself from the despotism of the first daughter-in-law and beginning to monopolize the old man's time, interest and fancy to the exclusion of his children and grandchildren.

The second son and his family lived in closest proximity to Meng Achoi and Xiao-li, and the arrival of seamstresses and jewellers vying for her patronage did not escape the women's notice. Forced to put up with these unwelcome changes, as they all depended on the financial support of Meng Achoi, they provided the rest of the clan with ammunition for gossip and conspiratorial intrigues. These increased in intensity as the concubine's hold over Meng Achoi grew stronger.

Xiao-li was aware of the hostility around her; she could scarcely have remained ignorant of it. Although she was the master's favourite, the management of the household remained in the first daughter-in-law's control, and that included the expenses incurred by Xiao-li. The master granted favours, but the money to secure these favours came from the daughter-in-law. What an opportunity for rekindling the ever-present conflict between the two women! The money incessantly requested by Xiao-li had to be deducted from the common household budget. The resentment of the women in the Meng family grew proportionately with Xiao-li's increasing appetite for luxury. The insatiable greed of an ill-educated outsider with no other involvement in the family – so it must have seemed – but lust for what it was felt should be spent on the rightful heirs, Xiao-li was hated. The women were Xiao-li's prime adversaries; they and their sons had everything to lose should the money cease to flow in their direction.

Not quite a year after Xiao-li had become a concubine, she gave birth to a daughter, Kam-yang, who was to remain her only child. The child grew up lonely, feeding upon the hostile atmosphere around her, which at times escalated into attempts at assassination. As the concubine was resented, so the child, too, was treated as a hated intruder.

Moot Xiao-li had known only one kind of permanence in her life: the power of money over people. The search for it had ruled her father's decision to sell her to Yip Min-yuk; the greed for profit had made Yip sell Xiao-li as a concubine, and now money and the possession of it enabled her to acquire undreamt-of luxuries.

Money became the key-symbol to a life marked by the search – itself deriving from her life's insecurity – for an elusive kind of power. But money was more than a symbol. It was also an obsessive fetish which in the end destroyed her own natal family and her child. In such a human context, people were reduced to mere instrumental value – having never experienced enduring human relationships, for Xiao-li people constituted only so many more transient factors in a cruel and competitive world.[33]

Thus Xiao-li was able to face the resentment around her with indifference, as the price to be paid in a competitive world. Ostracized by her jealous relations and their partisan friends and acquaintances, she continued to receive visits from her former fellow mooi-jai and from the daai-kam-je Yip Min-yuk, who had come to see herself as her successful protégée's foster-mother. At that time Xiao-li also began to institute enquiries as to the whereabouts of her family in Macau. The former mooi-jai, coming from a background of grim poverty and heightened aspirations – due to Yip Min-yuk's training – would have seen herself at the peak of material ambitions.

It was not uncommon, upon the death of the first wife, to make a favourite concubine a *tin-fong* (lit., to fill the chamber in place of the dead wife; indicative of a position commanding respect). Did Xiao-li's ambitions stop at the acquisition of concubine status or was Meng Achoi's respect of public opinion greater than his infatuation with the concubine? Men of Meng's class and wealth could keep women who fulfilled the single function of sex-objects. During Xiao-li's lifetime and with the growing dissolution of familial ties in 20th century Hong Kong, women who once would have been taken as concubines were set up in separate establishments and became known as 'black-market mistresses'. The fact that Xiao-li was instituted as a concubine made her no less a sex-object. Spoilt materially, she was never treated as a person who deserved respect and public recognition. Meng Achoi never sought to raise her level of learning and thus to diminish an important indicator (together with her unbound feet) of her inferior status. Xiao-li remained until the end of her life uncultured and illiterate, preoccupied with amassing private wealth. Although she was an attractive person, on a sexual level, her master disregarded her non-material requirements, that is, those aspects of her which would have shown concern for Xiao-li independent from the pleasure it gave to see her attractively dressed, decorated, and feasted.[34]

Among women, any pretension to rank which did not accord with her low background was quickly uncovered and viciously exposed to the public by other women of her circle. A young-looking woman in her forties was introduced to me after I had been given comprehensive instructions about the 'correct' behaviour towards her – I was to be friendly but distant. She had seduced and married a man about fifty years her senior when she was poor but attractive. Ten years and two children later, the man died, leaving her a young, wealthy widow. This in itself did not cause as much indignation (on the contrary, her 'luck' was talked of, as one good strategist discusses the techniques employed by a rival) as her refusal to associate with women from her former circle, whom she considered beneath her. It was the woman's refusal to be slotted into the role of a grateful, humble widow – grateful and humble towards other women in her new circle, thankful for the riches she so little deserved – and her insistence on furthering her own advancement without the legitimacy granted by breeding and education, which today still rankles among women acquaintances who can boast of breeding but little wealth. Similar characteristics can be detected in Xiao-li's lack of concern about the reaction of the Meng household towards her greed for material possessions. On the contrary, the more hostile the other women became, the more uninhibited grew Xiao-li's life-style.

Moot Xiao-li was never accepted into the women's circle in the Meng household, but considered merely a sexual appendage and looked upon with contempt. She was made to feel an intruder, and her life-style was put to me as having been a source of shame for the family. It was this outsider-status which must account for the adversaries' perception of the 'lawlessness' of such women as Xiao-li: if the concubine's interests do not coincide exclusively with those of the man's family, and if the material concern of future heirs is a matter of indifference to her, she will be concerned only with the well-being of outsiders like herself. Women like Xiao-li were regarded with suspicion and hostility; her heterodox behaviour constituted a threat to patriarchal assumptions about 'lawful authority', which it was in the interest of the other women, in their station of mother and wife, to defend. At this point the female (uterine) and male (patrilineal) foci merged to unite against the common enemy-outsider of whom Xiao-li was a 'typical' representative.[35]

Moot Xiao-li and her Natal Family

Once a Chinese bride had crossed the threshold of her bridegroom's house, she was assumed to have transferred allegiance from the father's to the husband's lineage. The severance of her ties with the natal family was symbolized by an emphatic shutting of the door after the bride. She entered the bridal sedan chair and, concealed behind red curtains, she emerged to the public eye only when, having travelled the obligatory *rite de passage*, she reached the walled courtyard of her bridegroom's home.[36] Of course, when the bride's new home was only a short distance away from her parents' home, she might visit them daily; yet, however close in distance, however good the relations with parents and brothers, public expectations dictated stronger identification with the interests of the conjugal home than with those of the natal family.[37]

In contrast, Xiao-li, as well as Margaret Leung's grandmother and the rival of Margaret's mother, the concubine (these women's histories appear later), took an extraordinarily close interest in the affairs and welfare of their blood-relatives, often to the detriment of their husbands' descendants.

Once Xiao-li had established herself as a concubine in Hong Kong she made every effort to trace her family. How she succeeded in finding them is not known. More than eight years had passed since her last contact with them. When the family was discovered, a turning-point had arrived in the life of its members. Interpretations of this turning-point differ, according to grand-daughter and great-grand-daughter, applying their respective perceptions of familial obligations and femaleness: whereas one interprets the event as the beginning of a time when Xiao-li could discharge her daughterly duties to her father and sisterly duties to her only brother, the other sees it as the 'beginning of the end', when the name of the family and their descendants were covered with 'disgrace and shame'.[38]

Xiao-li's father had not worked since the day he received payment for his daughter. The first daughter had been married off to an unknown man from the country, the rest of the family lived with their father. The youngest daughter was mentally retarded, and the only son, Moot So-ha, had become a work-shy and parasitic man, preferring to spend his time at the gambling-table rather than in supporting his family.

Subsequent to the discovery that the daughter who had been sold was now a wealthy concubine, members of the Moot family made regular appearances at the Meng house to demand their promised share. Father and brother were enabled by the monthly income to spend not only part of their time at the casinos but all of it. Xiao-li gave her brother money to buy a wife. The first wife had come from an unknown background but informants agree that at the time So-ha took her as a wife, she had worked as a prostitute, and that she was 'nice'. The unfortunate woman was barren and, after two years, when gambling-debts were piling up, So-ha had sold her. By granting him money to buy a second wife, Xiao-li gave her tacit consent to the sale. She also gave him money to start off a business in Macau, but before he set foot in Macau he had gambled and lost his whole starting capital in a game that had lasted from when the ferry left Hong Kong until it arrived in Macau harbour.

Xiao-li insisted that her generosity should be celebrated in an ostentatious manner. Despite the fact that her brother's first wife was still alive, a ceremony, customarily reserved for a wife only, was put on and the red-curtained sedan chair sent to fetch the new bride from a Macanese brothel. The incident was related to me as 'the mock-marriage'. This second union produced four children, three daughters and one son. At the end, only the son remained; the wife and her three daughters fell victim to Moot So-ha's gambling passion and recurrent streaks of ill-fated betting. When and how they were sold is not known, but one day Moot So-ha appeared in Hong Kong to ask for money; he wanted to buy out an expensive prostitute and lacked the necessary cash. Even the money he was paid for the sale of his daughters and his second wife had already evaporated.

So the brother made again his appearance at the Meng house, coming and going with awful regularity. 'He appeared in rags and left in riches'.[39] When he claimed that his wife had burned to death and that he needed the money for funeral expenses, even Xiao-li lost patience with him – not on moral grounds, but on grounds of his financial incompetence. Thus, the next time round she did not pay for a lavish marriage-ceremony. The prostitute joined So-ha as his third (and last) consort one dark evening, bringing her belongings on a wheel-barrow.

All three of Xiao-li's nieces were sold into prostitution in Macau. The fate of only one is known, and that only up to the time she one day arrived in Hong Kong with her lover; they were on their way to Singapore. Kam-yang remembers her heavily made-up cousin and the swarthy complexion of the man. It was rumoured that he was an important member of a secret society based in Singapore. The cousin was considered very lucky to have made such a catch but no one knows how long she kept the interest of her lover. She was not heard of again.

Moot So-ha's demands for money became more frequent. After Meng

Achoi's death (Kam-yang was then about ten years old), his insistent requests for cash were accompanied by threats of blackmail should Xiao-li not continue to support him. So-ha boasted of his criminal connections in Macau and warned of unpleasant consequences for the whole family were Xiao-li not to heed his admonitions. Nothing ever happened, so it may have been an empty threat. Xiao-li never failed to pay up, if with increasing reluctance. It had become clear to her how much of a liability So-ha would become to her daughter's future prospects of a respectable husband. Sometimes, so Kam-yang remembers, So-ha would sit in front of the house in dirty and shabby clothing (causing something of a commotion in a highly prestigious neighbourhood) until Xiao-li was compelled to remove him – with the help of a handsome cash bribe.

Still today, stories are told about Moot So-ha by descendants, suitably mythicized, depicting him both as a 'crawling beggar in rags' and as a 'dangerous hoodlum'. His perceived appearance depended on the effect the story-tellers wished to create on the listener. Eventually, So-ha came to Hong Kong to live in the basement of the Meng house; his third wife did some sewing for Xiao-li to earn their keep. On her deathbed, Xiao-li refused to see her brother, such was her wrath at his improper conduct. He died soon after.

So-ha was not the only person who figured prominently in the communications made to me about 'that low family' of Xiao-li. A wife rarely or never brought her family to live with the husband (this would be even more unthinkable if she were a concubine), but shortly after Xiao-li's discovery of her family's whereabouts, she took the sixth sister into the Meng household. Kam-yang, who was then about nine years old, remembers seeing her aunt ('Sixth Sister'), who was barely out of her teens, dressed in fine clothes; she lived in a space allocated to her on the verandah adjacent to Xiao-li's room. Xiao-li had decided that her sister should make a rich marriage. But the girl was 'wilful' and, falling in love with a handsome but comparatively poor younger cousin of Meng Achoi, she decided to marry him. As Kam-yang told me, the wedded pair assumed that Xiao-li would continue to support them as she supported the rest of the family in Macau.

'Sixth Sister' gave birth to seven children, all of whom died in infancy. After her death, the man remarried and his second wife gave birth to healthy offspring. Much was made of the dark symbolic forces at play in Sixth Sister's destiny and the shadow which lay over the whole Moot family.[40] That Xiao-li was able to take Sixth Sister to live with her, despite violent opposition from the rest of the household, says a great deal about the influence she had on Meng Achoi.

The generosity displayed towards the Moot family (albeit through Xiao-li) contrasted with Achoi's indifference to the fate of his only daughter, the child of his first concubine. Her husband had deserted his family to join a mistress on the mainland, and she and her children had been left penniless; yet Achoi provided her with very little financial support. The Meng family felt this to be an added insult, perpetrated by Xiao-li.

Shortly after Meng Achoi's death, the most notorious of a notorious family, Xiao-li's Youngest Sister, arrived. She was not only mentally retarded, but also a 'nymphomaniac' and Xiao-li did not discourage her from bringing in men from the street. As Helen Chan remarked to me, what a good thing it was that this youngest sister did not menstruate – she might have brought one bastard after the other into the world.

Xiao-li kept this youngest sister until her death, a few years later. Whenever I asked how her mental retardedness expressed itself it was put to me that she could think only of men and fine clothes and how to get satisfaction from them. She simply sponged off her elder sister's good fortune without, however, being able to turn it into security for herself. Her horizon was limited, and her initial simple-mindedness grew into a single-minded pursuit of her obsession with sex, luxuries and instant gratification – regardless of loss of face and the social repercussions of her actions on the family.

I wonder whether by mental retardation my informants meant those character-traits of the Youngest Sister which brought her into conflict with so many assumptions about 'shrewd' womanly behaviour? She lived recklessly, not planning her future which, if it was to be secure, had to be built around the construction of a nexus of family relationships. In fact, her character was the logical progression – in an extreme manifestation – of what, in a modified form, had been present in Xiao-li.

Today the last traces of the Moot family have vanished. In December 1978, Helen Chan went to Macau, to the hillside on which the shacks of the poor perch as precariously as ever. She found no one who could have told her about the Moot family. Fingers pointed vaguely in various directions. Standing there, Helen felt as remote from her great-grandparents as from the curious, poorly dressed squatters of whose world she knew nothing.

Descendants and Aftermath

A change in the status of a female was conditional on the intervention of a member of the male dominant structure. When Meng Achoi took Xiao-li as a concubine her status as mooi-jai was nominally nullified, but in fact, remnants of past oppression remained with her all her life. Meng Achoi changed her material existence: through him she acquired access to money and to the means to satisfy her expensive tastes; through him she was able to support her natal family. Through her, Meng Achoi gained a temporary illusion of youth and virility – and a daughter. Xiao-li's reward was the better part of the Meng fortune that, by rights, should have benefited his heirs.

Yet, while he granted her all that, he was content to withhold from her the protection and support needed to build up a position of dignity and recognition for herself, and ultimately her descendants, in relation to the rest of the household. In other words, the attributes of slavery changed – although her unbound feet would always proclaim her origins – but not the intimate parameters of its oppression: the world of women, the territory of a household, excluded the concubine from its inner circle. Viewed from the outside, Xiao-li had acquired membership of a respected and wealthy family, but from the inside, she remained an outcast on the domestic periphery. Although, by having taken Meng Achoi's fancy, Xiao-li possessed a virtual *carte blanche* in financial matters, her master's generosity went no further than what he considered the appropriate rewards for a pleasing sex object.

How does one measure regard, hostility, contempt in a relationship? The treatment that Xiao-li received at the hand of the Meng family never ceased to be a point of contention between her daughter and grand-daughter, and between these two and Meng's descendants.

The lines of combat in a household are set by circumstances outside the control of the individual participants, but the combatants may modify the rules and establish alliances which can result in tense power conflicts. Xiao-li was the favourite of the head of the household, but the domestic space was under the control of the first daughter-in-law and the women within her orbit of influence. Xiao-li's power may eventually have enabled her to undermine the position of superior wealth occupied by the Meng family, enriching herself and her dependants at their expense, but the coveted social status and privileges this wealth conferred upon her adversaries continued to elude her. Both Meng Achoi's indifference to her standing in the family, and the powerful familial opposition, came to overshadow the life of her daughter, Kam-yang.

Kam-yang remembers her childhood with a glow of defiant pride and idealized affection for father and mother. As the child of an outsider she was part of a smaller world than that circumscribed by the household *per se*; her world was anchored in the relationship with an ailing father and her mother. From her tenth year that world consisted of her mother and herself, supplemented by the social circle of her mother-concubine and Kam-yang's own school-friends.

Memory is selective, and Kam-yang's past is interwoven with a present that carries powerful emotions of pride, condescension, inferiority, and an overwhelming need for acceptance from her relatives.

Pride is rooted in her image of the father: powerful, shrewd, strong. A man of dignity and high standing in the Hong Kong community.

Oh, my relatives were always jealous of me, as far as I can remember they were jealous of me. Even as a small girl I was my father's favourite. I was a real tomboy, I was dressed like a boy and my father was proud of me. When important officials came to my house, my father would always take me and introduce me to them. I was such a nice and well-behaved girl.

Although Kam-yang relates with pride how much she meant to the father, in contrast to his disappointing sons, it is debatable whether he had as much time to spare for her as she would now like to believe. Ill and self-centred, in his better hours preoccupied with friends, his little daughter cannot have been quite the sole occupation of his life. From many remarks she made during the course of our talks, I gathered that her childhood was predominantly lonely. Not belonging to either world – neither that of her maternal nor that of her paternal kin – she came to distort the reality of her mother's past – by clothing it with a veneer of genteel respectability – and the actual standing of her father's family. She came to invest the latter with a mystery and glamour that were possible only because of the social distance that had always separated her from this, her source of pleasure and pain.

A vivid memory, which for her was somehow linked with a golden past, however imaginary, and with everything she wished to be an accepted part of, she related to me as a fragment from her early childhood:

Peering from the garden of her father's property, she would observe on the 15th of the eighth month a procession of richly-clad young ladies walking through the moonlit garden that belonged to a rich neighbour. On these occasions, in order to pay homage to the moon, they would wear traditional costumes exquisitely embroidered. The young ladies were followed by slave girls, also decked out in traditional garments. These slaves carried Chinese lanterns showing the way to a secluded spot where the company might converse and drink tea. The moon was entertained with music, laughter, and recitals of poetry.[40]

It is a memory precious to Kam-yang – precious, because she has only her vision of the 'golden past' to sustain her pride in the face of her daughter's constant aggressive attack on the questionable morality of her maternal family, and in the face of the persistent refusal from the members of the 'legitimate branch' to acknowledge Kam-yang's right to a joint illustrious family-legend, a myth both sides insist on:

As a little girl I liked to sit in the garden, you know, we had a very big garden, the gardeners looked after it very well. Everyone admired the many beautiful chrysanthemum flowers my father was so proud of.

When Chan Kam-yang reminisced about her youth she would often, in the midst of reveries about the happiness of those days, become agitated at the memory of her relatives' 'nastiness' in their treatment of her. The 'nastiness' covered attempts on the lives of both mother and daughter, involving arson, use of *fu*, paper-charms, and the participation of a spirit-medium and of a witch-doctor.

Once I sat on the stone-steps in the garden, when Johnny [Meng Achoi's third son's son] pushed me from behind and down the steps. I lost a tooth. He still daren't look me in the eye. Another time someone tried to topple a huge flower-pot from above and it nearly hit my head and killed me.

When she sat quietly in the garden, 'they' would come suddenly from behind and 'hiss at her', making her jump with fright. After the father's death, the last protection withdrawn, the persecution became worse. Sometimes she woke in the morning and would find under her pillow two of her own long hairs, tied together. On the two outer sides paper-images of *gwai* (demons) were attached.[41] These images were used in funerary rites. But in using them in the way related by Kam-yang, a sorceress had placed a spell on them to draw her into evil bondage; and to save her from madness,[42] her mother had to invoke a counter-spell. Kam-yang told me she had never been allowed time for herself when a young girl. But even when she was by herself, she lacked the peace for concentration on reading and writing. 'It is difficult in large Chinese families. Ba Jin told it so well. Much quarrel and strife goes on all the time.'

Kam-yang's relationship with her mother was central to her ideas and values, which had survived more than 70 years of social changes and cultural shifts in attitudes towards female roles and family life. The concubine, Xiao-li, transmitted to her daughter the values she had acquired in the course of her life (after Meng Achoi's death her influence was unchallenged) and Kam-yang was socialized into a reality of buyers and sellers. Those with power bought; those who were weak were bought. As long as Meng Achoi lived, sexual favours kept Xiao-li in a position of relative strength. After his death, money had to take over from sex to buy favours and approval. And so the concubine's daughter came to rely on money to preserve the cherished link, no less important for being built on dreams, with the milieu of her social superiors: the 'legitimate' side of her paternal family. Money here appears as a true manifestation of the alienation of human beings from themselves and therefore from others; it becomes the embodiment of all that is desirable and enviable about the life of others. Aspirations are concentrated on, and calculable in, so much investment, so much property, so much income – and human relationships, too, feature as a mere expression of this underlying value-system.

One of the favourite 'wicked persons' in the melodrama of Kam-yang's life was the first daughter-in-law who treated concubine and child with equal hostility. As with the daai-kam-je, her end was relished with glee by the tale-bearers: 'She died in a very bad way'. The 'bad way' to which my informants referred was the incident that had sparked off a major row in the daughter-in-law's family.

An obsessive gambler, on one occasion the first daughter-in-law had gambled away the unthinkable. On her death her children opened the ten trunks in which the death-garments of the deceased were kept, but were greatly shocked to discover the trunks were empty: the woman had literally gambled away her last shirt.[43] According to Chan Kam-yang, the deceased woman's children and grandchildren were so mean 'they made a great show of having to buy medicine to rub the corpse'. Xiao-li was asked to contribute from her riches. Thus Helen, appreciative of the deep irony of the outcome of this intervention by her grandmother, told me that the set of death-garments Xiao-li had prepared for herself was given to the dead arch-enemy. Whether this was done in a spirit of forgiveness or spite is not known.

Kam-yang's childhood and adolescence were undermined by the rejection of those people whom she looked up to and revered. With growing age this urge to become 'one of them', to be accepted, grew stronger. Her life when young was intimately tied up with that of her mother and her particular circle. She was more aware than her mother of the discriminations associated with a mooi-jai past, and more sensitive to the self-righteous superiority affected by the other women in the household. Today she idealizes her mother to such an extent that she has been transformed into a figure of saintly and refined dignity.

That this does not tally with other people's accounts of Xiao-li and with the inferences one must draw from her background and her conduct as an adult, is challenged by Kam-yang with the assertion that she knew her mother best and everything else said of her is prejudice. Much of Kam-yang's need to elevate her mother into something superior is part of the personal craving for an identity that can satisfy her obsessive projections of personal gentility, high class, and superior education. An unrefined and vulgar image of her mother would interfere with this mental construct.

In the young girl the tension was unresolved, expressing itself in rebellious acts towards the mother's world as well as that of the paternal kin.

In one of the rooms in Kam-yang's house, where I visited her often, I noticed the painting of Mu-lan, dressed in military armour, hung prominently over the chimney-piece. This female warrior, Mu-lan, features in many Chinese legends and folk-tales as a courageous and filial daughter who saved her family's honour by going into victorious battle on behalf of her aged father. It was a bad painting, but the subject-matter was obviously important to Kam-yang. Whenever we looked at this painting she would tell me about the exploits of her youth. In many ways, Kam-yang was not subject to the customary restraints which were commonly imposed upon a girl of her generation and her father's social status. When she talks about herself, it is with pride that she relates her youthful adventures:

You know, I was not like the average mademoiselle. My life was out of the ordinary. I had to be strong. I wore boyish clothing, I was always fighting with my cousins and with the brothers of my schoolmates. When I was only 16-years-old [circa 1918] I went to school on a motorbike. A really heavy bike, you know. All my friends went to school by chair, but I just flew past them. It wasn't one of these small bikes, you know, mopeds or whatever they are called. My mother didn't care, she had no time for me as she had to nurse my father. I zoomed past my class-mates and they were very envious. Only when I had a heavy accident, I lost four teeth, and I fainted, did my mother insist I should buy a mini-car, a fourwheeler. I never liked to wear jewellery, but I liked to own it. I don't like jewellery at all, but I liked to possess it, you know.[44]

Kam-yang went to all the right schools but seemed never to have shown much enthusiasm for academic work. She was far more interested in 'leaving her mark' on society. To be noticed in some way, so as to compensate for a constant, inner nagging sense of social inferiority.

Had her father been still alive, his status might have lent his youngest daughter some of the advantages enjoyed by a girl of the upper classes. But with his death, Kam-yang was dominated by her mother's world of concubines, gamblers, servants, and women of the daai-kam-je's position; no countervailing influence ever existed in her life.

Kam-yang moved even closer to her mother during the long years of litigation to establish the terms of Achoi's testament. This identification with her mother as the central person in her life was also an identification with the set of values and behaviour centred on Xaio-li's *leitmotif*: women must build their lives around the alliance of sex with power to acquire the security of money. So the grandmother advised the 12-year-old Helen Chan: 'if you marry an old man, you get rich'. That is how Helen remembers her grandmother, out to make money, shrewd in her ways, wise about the source of power for females without authority.

Materially Kam-yang had always been well-off. In the same way that Moot Xiao-li would demand luxuries for herself she granted her daughter's every wish. The mother's greed to possess and accumulate lifeless objects as a means to acquire the kind of security which relationships had not provided, taught the child to value proprietorship above everything else. The power that material possession had over the mother communicated itself to the child as a strategic imperative which brought to human behaviour certain logical consequences of action and attitudes: self-interest.

Not that Kam-yang expressed herself in this way. She preferred to maintain an aura of religious piety and to be judged in this vein by others. Charged with religious guidance, her pronouncements on the state of the world acquired the dogmatic quality of a papal pronouncement; and as unassailable. Yet her religious sources are nothing if not eclectic. The mother was 'a very devout Buddhist'.[45] Kam-yang considers herself to be a Protestant, but in her assessment of human society the guiding principles are distinctly derivative of Confucianism, coloured by Buddhist notions of rewards and punishment, enriched by Christian beliefs of heaven and hell.[46] Kam-yang is also not averse to utilizing a spirit-medium if and when the occasion demands it.[47] She believes in a Supreme Being, but does not care what it is called. Age increases the influence of enunciated Confucianist principles pertaining to the treatment of elders and superiors.[48]

The daughter, Helen, prefers to cultivate an attitude of cynicism towards religion and piety. Having observed her grandmother's and mother's religious sentiments in action, she considers herself at best an agnostic, preferably an atheist. But she respects old traditions and customs in order not to hurt 'other people's feelings on religion'. She is, therefore, motivated out of consideration for others, making a point of participating in funerary rites and anniversary celebrations, paying New Year visits and distributing red packets of 'good luck money' if appropriate.

As I said earlier, Kam-yang was socialized into a world of conflicting demands and aspirations and she reacted by modelling herself on heroic and victorious prototypes from literature and legends typifying successful challenges to life's adversities. Thus she created for herself the role of a courageous heroine who defended her mother from the attacks of her hostile relatives. Kam-yang had ample opportunities during 30 years of litigious family feuds to prove her fettle.

When Meng Achoi died in 1911, the concubine Xiao-li was still only in her mid-twenties; her daughter Kam-yang was about ten years old. I was told by Chan Kam-yang that yellow papers were pasted on the façade of the house, bearing the names of the bereaved. Her mother's and her own name were among the relatives' names listed. This fact was to prove an important substantiating factor in Kam-yang's fight to defend her mother's legal rights.

The mourning period provided only a superficial kind of truce between Xiao-li and her daughter, and the rest of the household. When the terms of the testament became known this threadbare civility ended. Tacit animosity broke out into open warfare that was to last more than 30 years, for 20 of which the parties had to suffer each other's presence under one roof. The Will had stipulated that the properties must neither be alienated nor divided.

The history of the family feud is long and tortuous. So bitter was the quarrel that I neither expected nor indeed encountered any measure of objectivity among my informants from either side. Yet these subjective interpretations are invaluable, because they tell much about the participants' conflicting perceptions of each other and go some way towards illuminating present-day undercurrents of mutual dislike and taciturn distrust.

The seeds of conflict were sown when in a final Will Meng Achoi appointed Xiao-li as his chief executrix. In an earlier draft he had appointed two of his sons, but the final version superseded this draft. The descendants of the wife and the first concubine maintain today that the change of will was due to 'evil influences' brought upon an old and impressionable man by his scheming concubine. Xiao-li's daughter's version gives as the reason Meng Achoi's disappointment with these two sons: they turned out to be swindlers and small-time clerks. Because they had misused their father's trust he relied on his beloved concubine, Xiao-li, instead.

Co-executors of the Will were the wife of the fourth son – who had disappeared to Macau and under false pretences married a Macanese woman as his rightful wife – and a 'weak son' who possessed little authority. The reason given to me for the inclusion of the fourth son's wife was that in the two years preceding Meng Achoi's death, she had been treated badly by her family. She had little money, and her constant begging for more help hardly endeared her to her money-conscious relatives. She then turned for help to Xiao-li, 'flattering her', according to Helen Chan, and making her feel that being wooed by a formerly hostile member of the 'other side' increased her importance. Thus Xiao-li suggested to Meng Achoi that her name should be included in the list of executors; in this she succeeded.

What happened in the two years after Meng Achoi's death is unclear. Descendants of the main branch of the family maintain that the two women completely mismanaged the estate and that two ignorant and illiterate women attempting to manage a complex estate were bound to run into trouble. Chan Kam-yang asserts her mother had problems in 'getting the right legal help' and was thus helpless in the hands of 'sharks' who exploited a fertile source of income. Also, the rest of the family was jealous and found the thought of Xiao-li occupying such an authoritative position unbearable.

In 1913 two court cases made judgement on the construction of the Will; the first in a long sequence of trials which benefited only lawyers and clerks. Vast sums of money were spent on bribery to influence the course of justice.

The Meng family contended that Xiao-li was not a concubine but a mistress and that her daughter had no right to a dowry as stipulated by Meng Achoi. The defendants cited the customary rites which had accompanied Xiao-li's entry into the family, and the funerary papers that had clearly carried the name of the descendant Kam-yang. The reference in legal documents to 'the single woman' Xiao-li was not discovered until a few years later when Kam-yang perused the documents submitted by the Meng family.

At some point in time the eldest sons of Achoi took over the *de facto* management of the estate. According to Kam-yang, when she was 14 years old, she fought for her mother and for the rights of the fourth son's wife, like her model-heroine Mu-lan, fearlessly and courageously. One may entertain a certain degree of scepticism as to the ability of a teen-age girl to understand the complexities of legal entanglements. Some of her stories were simply incredible.

One of the incidents concerned 'the intimidating practices' of her relatives. Kam-yang would at times call family-meetings with all the members – constituting on occasion as many as four branches – present.

The atmosphere was so emotionally loaded that some people carried daggers in their belts. She was not frightened, so Kam-yang proudly told me; she stood up to them and admonished the young men that 'this was not the place to fight', the real fight would be held in the courts.

Whatever the factual reality of those 30 years, the litigation devoured vast sums of money from the family estate and in the end left comparatively little to Kam-yang, and even less to her relatives. More fatal still were the lasting fissures between the 'legitimate' and the 'illegitimate' branch. Today the wounds are still unhealed. Lineage banquets and the like, which I attended with Chan Kam-yang and her daughter, provided visible evidence of the perpetuation of the breach. The dissimilarity of the respective members' fortunes is not easily forgotten or ignored and the origin of the two women, Kam-yang and her daughter, is never far from the consciousness of all Meng descendants. The mooi-jai institution was abolished in 1923 (see below) but its underlying social evaluations and attitudes have survived, to be reckoned with today as much as yesterday.

Growing up under the auspices of her mother, to contract an advantageous match became the central goal of Kam-yang's life. At the relatively late age of 29 years, when most women of her generation had been mothers for several years, Kam-yang married a medical student, an 'outsider' in terms of Hong Kong society, from a humble Indonesian background. In the context of the two women's social ambitions this marriage can in no way have approximated to their aspirations. The reasons for this marriage become intelligible, however, when one realizes that Xiao-li's social circle and particular reputation had prejudiced Kam-yang's chance of marrying into Hong Kong's exclusive upper echelon. The mother's background was there for all to see, and the Meng household doubtless added their own brand of gossip about the unsavoury origins of the concubine.

Lack of physical attractions prevented Kam-yang from following in her mother's footsteps. Her pallor was sickly and she suffered from tuberculosis. By the time John Chan arrived in their world, he was found to be an adequate catch for Kam-yang. Although not a member of the Hong Kong social élite, he nevertheless held out the future promise of a lucrative medical practice. The standing enjoyed by a medical doctor in Chinese society was high enough to make up for other deficiencies of wealth and native status. This consideration motivated Xiao-li to resort to her well-tried tactics of resolving human problems by pecuniary means. When Kam-yang met John Chan, they were both at the University of Hong Kong. Kam-yang soon dropped out, John Chan struggled on with the little money he received from his family. Kam-yang's mother invited him to the comfort of her home and offered to help him out by meeting his accumulated debts.

Soon, offers of material assistance turned into massive obligations for John Chan. The more money he accepted the heavier the burden of repayment. As time went by, his visits to the Meng house became more frequent, and again, the household was rife with speculation about the goings-on in Xiao-li's family.

It is said that before John Chan realized the exact nature of the connection he was to seal by the marriage vows, he was too deeply committed to his future mother-in-law to extricate himself honourably. He was weak and easily impressed by the display of wealth and class, but he was also a man of honour and real kindness and, according to his daughter, totally unprepared for his wife's grasping and possessive nature. His widow's testimony says that he married her only to 'get on in the world' and then deserted her for 'low women'. Probably both interpretations have a grain of truth in them.

The marriage proved to be a disaster. Xiao-li's influence on the young couple and her constant presence intensified Chan's opposition to the Meng household. After his return from the honeymoon he met Kam-yang's maternal uncle and his mistress, both of whom had just moved into the basement. Coming from a poor but 'honest background' Chan was a stranger to such a milieu. His mother, twice widowed, had brought up her ten children by running a bakery in Java, 'without selling one of her offspring'.[49] The marriage of Kam-yang and John Chan had begun inauspiciously and proved to be a tragedy for them and their child, Helen.

Once he had opened a surgery and begun to do well, John Chan gradually removed himself from his wife's household. Bitter conflicts over money and his absence from the home invariably affected their child, whom each used as a pawn to strike at the other in their conjugal battles. The irony was bitter for Chan Kam-yang. What she had condoned in her mother and defended in the legal battle still raging at that time, she now attacked bitterly from the position of a wronged wife. She was now on the 'legitimate side'. It was Chan Kam-yang who talked to me with disgust about her husband 'ensnared by common tarts'. When her daughter pointed out to her, in my presence, how contradictory she was in her positions on the rights of wives and concubines, Chan Kam-yang defended herself by making a distinction between defined sets of behaviour expected from members of differing social classes. Her husband had been a professional man and should have pursued higher standards rather than playing with prostitutes, and contracting syphilis. The maternal uncle had been a common man and low-class, he did not know better. Her husband's behaviour must be judged with more stringent criteria. When he died she discovered that his testicles were swollen to double their normal size. According to her this was due to stimulants to make him 'perform better'.

When John Chan spent his money on women and pleasures outside the home Kam-yang revenged herself by refusing to divorce him. He had set up a mistress who bore him several sons; their existence has never been recognized by Kam-yang. While she could not challenge his way of life outright, Kam-yang used her child, and her refusal to divorce him, to make her bitter opposition known to her husband. When she told me that all her fierce opposition had been 'for the good of the child', Helen laughed and dismissed this as a cheap argument: the argument of a defeated wife.

During interviews, mother and daughter never talked – they abused each other. Helen defends her father as weak but good, driven to excesses only by the behaviour of his mother-in-law and his wife. What she cannot forgive, on the other hand, is her mother's exploitation of the child to get money out of the husband; to capitalize on the child's appeal and make the father's remorse benefit her purse. 'Why could she not fight her own battles?' The daughter, Helen Chan, still feels hurt and resentful towards her mother and grandmother whom she holds responsible for poisoning her childhood.

Chan Kam-yang accuses her late husband of having manipulated her daughter to oppose the mother, making her 'suffer for 30 years', and in the end giving everything to prostitutes, leaving her 'destitute'. When John Chan died, he left Kam-yang 'not a penny'. Valuable property had been wasted on the 'large-footed woman' (the mistress). 'Even now these women are collecting rents on the property, I know all about it.' Only the house into which Kam-yang and her mother had moved after the end of the litigation, in the late 1930s, had not been handed over 'to those prostitutes'; but neither had the house been given to Kam-yang. To her great humiliation the house, in which I interviewed mother and daughter over the long months of 1978, had been willed to Helen, who still owns it.

As a young child Kam-yang reacted ambivalently to her origins: there was the defensive identification with her mother, but also rebellion against both her maternal and paternal backgrounds. The adult Kam-yang, desperately seeking social acceptance and admission into an exclusive milieu, developed snobbish attitudes towards those whom she feared might contaminate her with 'low class', keeping an all-important social distance and, at the same time, she began to construct a whole mythology of the genteel poverty of her maternal kin. This idealization of her mother's history became easier as time went by and 'undesirable kin' died or just vanished; the remaining relatives were bought-off to prevent further social embarrassment.

Kam-yang persuades the paternal kin to attend her invitations by offering the enticements of good food, lavish entertainment and generous hospitality. She is invited in return, because she holds out the prospect of large contributions to dinner expenses and entertainment. Her money packets are always well-filled.

That is how the impoverished legitimate line gets its own back, Helen told me. Kam-yang is more vulnerable, socially, than was her mother – more desperate to belong to the family. While Xiao-li had pursued her aim with indifference to the family's reaction, Kam-yang's fight was, and is, a different one. As a first wife she was threatened by an outsider-mistress and mobilized all the righteousness of the member of a class that considered its rightful privileges threatened. Unlike Xiao-li she had started out on the defensive. Her husband's mistress not only impaired her rights as first wife, but also her reputation among those she wanted to impress. In the end, this was to mean distributing money. As her daughter, Helen, remarked uncharitably, it became a kind of redistribution of the wealth which the family had lost to Kam-yang's mother. Helen has taken up the cause of the Meng family. In her mind, the mother merges with the grandmother and the unsavouriness of the Moot background. She confided to me that she believes that, had her father died early, she too might have been sold, as her mother was too deeply steeped in 'that kind of life' to be trusted not to exploit an opportunity for making money. As Helen told me:

> In Chinese history one hears of such foolish girls who sell themselves to pay for a parent's funeral expenses and medical treatment; but at least there was filial piety there. With my grandmother's family there was only greed. Humans were so much commodity.
> What is the use of being 'a pious Buddhist' when you reduce your flesh and blood to goods? It is easy to pray to Buddha for luck and money; my grandmother was single-minded and sought to use religion for her own ends. Her deeds are one thing, the piety in real life is quite another.

In the course of many interviews I came to realize that it was the relationship between mother and daughter that determined the structure of the situation and, therefore, of our conversations. Very rarely did I get the opportunity to speak and listen to the mother without the daughter interrupting, and vice versa. A multitude of factors was responsible for the tension, and diversity of opinion and outlook. What made these interviews fascinating, if somewhat of a strain, was the fact that I was dealing not only with one specific relationship, but with the relationship of two persons who were also representatives of historical changes in the position of Chinese women.

The typical interview ended in a shouting-match between the two women; their respective opinions, loudly voiced, were ostensibly addressed to me, but in reality destined for the other who appeared never to listen; nevertheless, they knew exactly what the other was saying and were always ready to contradict each other. The issues were invariably linked with Xiao-li's past, her dealings in mooi-jai, her tacit approval of the sale and prostitution of her nieces, her impact on the Meng family, Chan Kam-yang's relationship with her husband, and the reality of The Myth, propagated by Chan Kam-yang about her past.

While Kam-yang would strongly defend her parents' name, and in bitter tones, accuse her daughter of unfilial behaviour and lack of understanding for anything to do with Chinese customs and traditions, Helen retorted in her own way: that Kam-yang, her mother, lived in a world of fantasy of her own making, that she was tainted by the long association with her vulgar and low-class mother, and that this had hardened her, making her prone to deviousness and secretiveness.

The central dilemma in Kam-yang's life was the question of allegiance to a particular class and social status. She never resolved this dilemma. This was clearly manifest in her own split personality. She had education and background, but the education had been superficial and the background precariously balanced between acceptance and rejection on the part of her paternal relatives.

Helen was sufficiently remote from her grandmother's mooi-jai status to allow for a sense of detachment to be developed, if not the noisy hostility which she herself calls objectivity. Although painfully aware of her grandmother's reputation and her mother's pretensions and social gyrations, she became more fully integrated into her class and, by virtue of an excellent education, secure enough to want to 'uncover the evils of the past'. That was how she would constantly refer to her grandmother and mother.

Helen had been educated at a convent school in Hong Kong, and after finishing school she left for Europe to take higher degrees in geography and literature. Her moral sensibility was formed by the educational experience and by her father, to whom she felt extremely close. She exorcises her mother's influence by cultivating friendships outside the family-circle, friends who 'belong only to her'. She would like to refuse to be involved in family quarrels and social meetings, or so she says, but her detachment is more apparent than real, if due only to a reluctance to relinquish opportunities to make succinct criticisms about her mother. To preserve her autonomy, she identifies strongly with the values acquired through Western education, and interprets traditional Chinese family life – as epitomized by her family – as oppressive and negative for the individual within it. In the course of her adult years the conviction has grown that the history of the Meng family can be seen only in one light – the darkest. In contrast, she is able to harbour strong emotions for people she can regard as antithetical to her mother and grandmother.

When Helen was a young girl, large parties were held in her honour; she has ceased to give or attend parties. She lives, reluctantly, in the large house left by her father and supervises the servants, writes letters, quarrels and broods over the past. Her life is monotonous, locked in daily confrontation with her mother. This love-and-hate relationship has left its mark on the daughter. Any incident, even the most trivial, gives rise to more accusations and counter-accusations that without fail stretch back to the past.

The estrangement of her parents and her own misery as a child made Helen look early at the society her father moved in. She saw how his gullibility was turned to good use by people who needed just such a dupe to invest in crazy schemes, to contribute to expensive but prestigious projects, to give lavish entertainments. Helen saw her father and mother bow to people who had only come to partake in free food and drink. She realized the extensive hypocrisy that prevailed in these social circles and the materialistic fetishism of Hong Kong society. Whether she was already like this as a teenage girl, whether these were rationalizations to justify her withdrawal from society as an adult, is difficult to establish. In the 1950s she was a much-noted figure in social diary columns of the Hong Kong press. While her mother would have given everything to have been noticed, her daughter distanced herself and looked with disdain upon the folly around her.

There is another side to Helen's life, a side of which she is little aware. Helen may view society in Hong Kong as an anathema, but her daily life is intricately tied up with it. An old friend, describing Helen's life, put it bluntly: 'she is trapped'. As a child she was cosseted and sheltered from material want. What she lacked emotionally was made up in material comfort. Servants attended to her every wishe, her mother surrounded her with all the paraphernalia suitable for her child. What John Chan was loath to grant his wife, he did not grudge his child: from a swimming-pool to European excursions, she was spoilt with lavish gifts. Her natural perceptive intelligence did not find its counterpart in practical application. Her theoretical rejection of everything her family stood for always remained an abstraction. Having never been granted the space to develop independence, her temperament was not matched by the strength required to persevere in a life style different from her mother's.

With middle-age the psychological pressures are acute. Distaste for her mother's conduct remains. She observes her mother and interprets her in the light of her version of the past. The sense of revulsion felt is expressed in obsessive, neurotic cleanliness that does not trust servants to eliminate the 'dirt' in the house for which she holds her mother responsible. Dirt has become Helen's constant source of irritability and criticism towards the mother, of nervous depression, of contempt that uses a secondary cause to attack the underlying roots of ever-present family tensions.

To her, the mother *is* dirt. That is, according to Helen, she is stained with the guilt and perversities of a slave's outrage on a family. The act of cleaning has become a daily ritual to wipe away the 'slovenliness' of the Moot past and to counter an inner, if subconscious, anxiety that she herself may, unwittingly and irreversibly, have been polluted.[50]

2. Old To, the 'Xiang Fei'

'Old To' was still alive in 1978. She was born during the late 1880s in an unknown village close to Macau – in the former Heungshan, now Zhongshan district.[51] Much less is known about her early life than about Moot Xiao-li's. Old To, as she is commonly called, was always very secretive about the exact circumstances of her first sale and very sensitive to any reference to her natal family; her 'low past' would have interfered with the image she wanted to project as a proud and powerful concubine. Also, the relationship with her husband's family was so tense that the surviving descendants are loath to discuss her; but when they do, it is with a vengefulness I have rarely encountered in a Chinese family.

When Old To was six or seven years old, her family sold her as a mooi-jai to a wealthy household in Macau. Her father had been an agricultural worker whose earnings were not enough to feed his large family; so the daughters were the first to go. Macau was near to their village and known to Chinese from the rural areas as a place where people still had enough money to pay for young females. (But this was only true for a small segment of the Chinese population. The majority, as in Hong Kong, lived from hand to mouth.) A go-between in Macau took the girl and said she knew of a family which might well need a mooi-jai. A few days later the negotiations were complete and the parties signed the *sung-tip*, a deed of sale giving unconditional rights of ownership to the family.

The Purchasers and the Mooi-jai

Old To was unlucky in being bought by a family that was constantly on the brink of financial disaster. The head of the family was a small merchant whose debts had made him seek refuge in opium- and gambling-houses. The more he smoked, the less he cared about the business, the more debts he incurred. Whether, in different circumstances, the family would have kept the girl one does not know. When the mooi-jai was about ten years old and instant cash was required to pay for the merchant's opium, he offered her to the owner of the opium den he frequented. This time the girl changed hands without any great formality and was used to serve the opium-pipes

CHART 5

'Old To' and her family

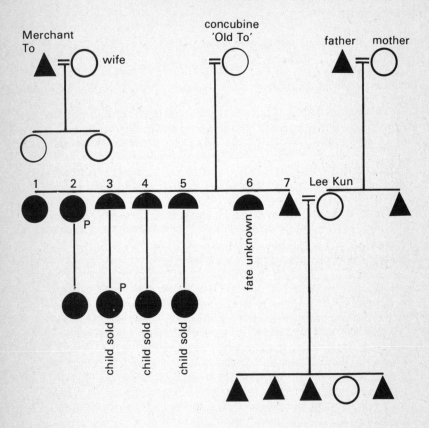

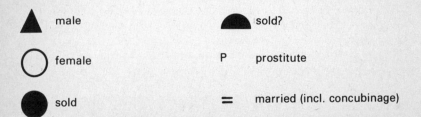

and entertain clients. She had become a marketable commodity, with a price like any other.

Here, I am not posing clear-cut opposites, for example, an intrinsically valued daughter as against To, the commodity. Chinese dominant perceptions of female nature (and for that matter, of male nature) scarcely provided for such existentialist grasp of human nature. But I suggest that Old To, in her standing as daughter, sister, and niece, had been a member of a social unit that provided validity and an affirmation of her existence that went beyond the commercial exploitation of a commodity, owned and alienable. It is on this point that I take exception to writers on Chinese women who fail to distinguish between an objectively perceived social system (which relegated women to a position of inferiority) and the manifold social parameters that allowed women so many relative differences in self-perception and social standing: the difference between To as daughter and To as a mooi-jai and an entertainer in an opium den, for example.

Nothing certain is known about the sort of man the proprietor of the opium den had been. It was a higher-class den because it was frequented by the wealthier merchants, and competitive pressure must have been great. Macau could boast of many opium-smokers: it was considered to be 'at the heart of the greatest nation of opium smokers in the world',[52] and many dens vied for the clientele. Women entertainers were part of the initial attractions; once a client, the nature of addiction to opium would create its own demands.

When Old To was first sold, to become a mooi-jai, she found herself with just one old family servant to share the heavy physical work. With the financial situation becoming progressively worse, the mooi-jai was compelled to take on more and more duties. Nothing could have been further from the theoretical position of a mooi-jai in 'an adoptive family' than the actual use of To as a work-horse. Her drudgery was of the heaviest – and the memory of her own childhood fading inexorably. Did she stop to think over her parents' action? She did not, like Moot Xiao-li, seek her family later; did this mark resentment? I do not know if it was truly poverty that made the father sell her. Macau's social history is stained with a long history of human trafficking, despite ineffectual attempts by the Portuguese colonial administration and the church to stem the trade.[53] The freely available opportunities for gambling and smoking, coupled with the harsh realities of life in and around Macau, certainly made the temptations hard to resist. The sale of daughters and wives was a logical outgrowth of a situation where the dispossessed, in order to get their share of Macau's pleasure industry, could barter little else than what they could dispose of by patriarchal authority. At this juncture sexual evaluations and cultural priorities merged with factors of class and economic disparities.

After the heavy drudgery at the merchant's house the opium den might have seemed preferable. Old To was good at entertaining clients and coaxing them ever deeper into opium and gambling debts. What she received from them she would keep for herself to buy opium and jewellery. She acquired a taste for gambling tables and the life-style which saw no further than the next pipe and the next game. She was successful in her way and could have saved money (to buy herself out), but she was so heavily indebted to the owner (commonly a deliberate policy on the part of the owner, as it was in brothels), that only a rich client could do this for her. By the time this happened she was nearly 15 years old and hardened by experience of the use and abuse of her person. She knew no kin and met those who mattered in her world (her clients) on a level at which emotional attachments were displaced by speculations of a kind that aimed at a client's purse and susceptibility.

Her perception of familial ties was tinted by her personal experience, and the daily encounters with wreckages of once proud lineages. Daily ferries between Hong Kong and Macau, and Guangzhou and Macau, ensured that many scions of wealthy Chinese families in those cities could enjoy the facilities Macau had to offer. In practically all the upper-class (and to some extent middle-class) Chinese families I interviewed in Hong Kong, one or several members of the family had been (and some still are) compulsive members of the gambling fraternity in Macau. Many Hong Kong residents owned houses in Macau which men often used as a refuge from familial constraints.[54] This was how the merchant To came to Macau on his regular trips and encountered the entertainer in his old opium haunt. When she was 15 years old and new supplies of girls brought fresher faces, she was sold to the merchant To as a concubine.

The 'Xiang Fei'

Merchant To's wife was not consulted. But being of a meek disposition, she gave her consent without much resistance. The To household in Hong Kong comprised then the ageing wife and two daughters. In the shortest time possible the man's affections, financial investments, and attention, had been transferred from his family to the concubine. The concubine encountered only feeble opposition from the mother and two daughters; according to the daughters she ruled everyone with an 'iron hand', and was ruthlessly determined to reap the material benefits from the family fortune for herself alone. Thus she acquired the nickname of Xiang Fei. Not long after Old To's appearance, the merchant's wife committed suicide by poisoning. The daughters maintain today that their mother was driven to death, as the Xiang Fei would tolerate no rivals to the master's heart and purse. She had been nicknamed Xiang Fei because her victims thought her to be very much like the notorious concubine Xiang Fei of Emperor Gaozong of the Qing dynasty. That concubine had enjoyed a popular reputation for her ruthless ambition and scheming nature – 'Old To', so I was told, could have been her sister.[55]

When still alive, the wife was so powerless that she could not assert her customary rights. The husband had turned his back on her and thus deprived her of the privileges derived from a husband's recognition of a wife's standing; the wife had come from a respected family in Guangdong, but relations with that family had long been cut off. The wife had only two daughters, even more helpless than their mother, and no son who might have contested her rights. A combination of these external factors, together with the woman's conventional upbringing, contributed to her vulnerability in the face of an independent and battle-hardened outsider. On available evidence it seems plausible that the wife was driven to suicide; but opposed to this interpretation is the fact that given her passive mentality she probably met the vicissitudes of fate with submission and resignation.

The concubine gave birth to seven children, five of them sons; her victory over the wife was total. Her relationship with the two step-daughters remained hostile and as soon as possible they were married off. The concubine did not wish to waste valuable money on them. Her own children were not treated with any more compassion. At best she brought them up with indifference. Emotional neglect and an inability to relate to them was to characterize her relationship with her children in times to come.

The concubine was given *carte blanche* by the merchant To to do with the money as she pleased; she spent it on gambling, smoking, and drinking. She had persuaded the merchant to set up home in Macau for part of the year, and there the daily routine rarely changed. She would get up late and leave the house to return late and often drunk. Frequently she gambled away the jewellery she wore on her person. When the husband reprimanded her for her life-style she knew how to pacify him. It was now her turn to be served, to be pampered with money and attention – and her turn to give orders and exploit those in her power.

Old To was in her early 30s when the merchant died, leaving her in full control of family and estate. The last restrictions lifted, she was seen at home only to change clothing, to get a few hours of sleep, and to replenish her supply of money. In time she was forced to sell her husband's shares and properties, her jewellery and other trinkets, in order to finance her increasing expenditure. One day, unable to meet gambling debts, she turned her first daughter-in-law into cash in Macau. Then it was the turn of her second daughter, who was sold into prostitution in Hong Kong. Old To ended up selling her daughters-in-law (three sons of hers had married in the meantime) and even overruled the sons' objections to the sale of the grandchildren (see Chart 6). What eventually happened to the four older sons is difficult to establish. One informant claims that they were also sold, another maintains that they ran away to start a new existence on the mainland.

Sons were considered precious in Chinese society and their disposal by the mother, Old To, shows how at odds an outsider's values can be with the official doctrine, for example, those values underlying the institution of ancestral worship. Old To's life was rooted in the imperatives of her egoistical priorities, antithetical to the priorities of women who seek security through the formation of uterine ties.

Only the youngest son remained with Old To as insurance against old age and infirmity, and in 1978 he was still slavishly devoted to her. It is otherwise with the youngest son's wife, who was so ill-treated and humiliated by her mother-in-law that she would often go to a friend of her parents to cry. She would have run away a long time ago but was warned that the children, especially the daughter, might be sold in her absence; so she remained. Her mother bitterly lamented to me her responsibility for allowing their only daughter to contract such an unhappy marriage. Old To has become a by-word for evil in their circle, which consists of plain farming-people based in the Hong Kong New Territories.

Here the psychological costs of enslavement were particularly pronounced and created terrible havoc with the lives of individuals subjected to Old To's rule. But she lived and acted within a system that was not of her own making; when she dared to act against an oppressive fate, her behaviour was pronounced an act of moral outrage: condemned in its expression of female independence as much as in its violation of ethical conduct.

Old Age

It happened that interviews with former mooi-jai were cancelled, or not permitted in the first place, because the mooi-jai issue was considered sensitive enough after all these years to merit the protection of an old mother or aunt from the curiosity of an outsider historian. But this case was different.

Although Old To had married into a wealthy family with some standing in Hong Kong and Macau, she now vegetates in a small wooden hut on a hillside overlooking Aberdeen reservoir in Hong Kong. There, with great reluctance, she is cared for by the mother of her ill-treated daughter-in-law. All that is left of her family are the youngest son and his family. The hut is part of a small farmstead owned by the Lee family – the son's wife's parents – and the son, with his family, lives there too. It is said that his miserliness is such that he begrudges the nominal rent he pays to his parents-in-law.

He treats his parents-in-law with contempt. For him they are rustic, ignorant people who do not appreciate the honour of supporting his family. The fact that, as the daughter-in-law refuses to come near her, the old Lee couple care for the old mother, that they look after the children when they come home from school, and feed the whole family from a well-tended vegetable plot, does not impress him. His mother made him feel he had married beneath him and he never objected when she treated his wife like a work-horse that needed to be beaten and put on meagre food-rations in order to perform her task in a suitably meek fashion.

Kun, the daughter-in-law, cried often and wanted to leave her family.

Every day she was obliged to listen to tales about her husband's great family and the golden past and riches that had once been theirs. Kun's share in the To family's 'golden past' consisted of hard words and the humiliation of her natal family. But it was to her own family she went for help when the money did not buy enough food for the children because her mother-in-law had appropriated it for herself.

Old To neither lifted a finger in her son's household nor showed much interest in her grandchildren. Only sometimes, when she stayed at home because the money for gambling had run out, or she had to recuperate from the excess of drinking, she would call her grandchildren and fill their ears with stories about their paternal origins that satisfied her own need for innate superiority over the Lee family, turned her dependence on them into rightful tributes, and the Lees into servile tributaries. Through her subjective vision the children came to see, and believe in, the social and cultural disparity between their mother's and father's respective origins. They listened to Old To's stories about herself as a brilliant and successful courtesan in Macau with a high-class clientele of her own choosing. She told them about celebrated occasions when she and her husband threw open the doors to welcome the society of Hong Kong. How through tricks and cunning their family was deprived of fortune and position, and how their father contracted a mésalliance which must shame his ancestors and downgrade the importance of his family line.

Thus it came that the grandchildren, too, began to look down on their maternal grandparents, treating them and their mother as servants. The grandmother told me how much she suffered from the aggressive and contemptuous behaviour of her eldest grandson, who had become impossible to control at home! His father, where it concerns his family's standing with the Lee family, does not interfere on principle. Cold and ungiving in relation to others, when it concerns his mother, he is a most slavishly devoted son. The old woman is now incontinent but has to lie in her excrement until the evening when the son comes home to clean her, to empty the chamber-pot, and to feed her. She, who used to be so fastidious in her life-style, now lives in a room that once was a pigsty.

I visited Old To on a hot and humid summer's day. When I opened the door the stench so overwhelmed me that I had to sit down. An old fan stood impotently in the corner, for ever unrepaired. The room was stuffed with a few bits of old furniture, a small altar with burnt-up joss sticks occupied a dark niche. Yellowed photographs on a small table were collecting dust below the altar. The old woman, then in her 90s, sat cross-legged on the bed, slowly fanning herself with an incongruously flamboyant fan of long, black feathers. She wore the ubiquitous grey pyjama-suit.

In the unbearably hot and oppressive atmosphere of the room the bustle and noise of Hong Kong outside seemed very far away. Here she had lived, immobilized, for nearly 20 years; dying slowly, too slowly for her daughter-in-law. Bitterness and resentment at the mother-in-law's treatment of her had turned into such strong revulsion that nothing and no one could make her go near Old To's room. And thus the old woman's last days were spent in self-induced isolation. Most of her former companions of past drinking-and-gambling days had long since died or were too infirm to make the difficult journey to the farmstead.

But probably Old To would have shown little interest in such visitors. The years had taken their toll and the world of her imagined past was more real than events taking place around her. She addressed herself only to the son, to complain about her conditions, lamenting the absence of servants she had long been unable to afford. She feigned not to notice old Mrs Lee who brought her midday rice. When I sat in the small courtyard enjoying the cool breeze under the big mango tree and a refreshing cup of tea I heard monotonous muttering coming from Old To's room. Old Mrs Lee sat down beside me and shook her head.

'My daughter doesn't like me to go in there, she would let her starve to death.' She listened. 'Poor woman,' she said. And indeed, the proud and defiant concubine of the past bore little resemblance to the old, 'poor woman' I remembered so vividly from my visit.

3. Margaret Leung's Grandmother

When I met Margaret Leung in Hong Kong in 1978, she was in her late 40s. Before I encountered her personally I had heard about her eccentricity, generosity, and extraordinary background and family history from a family friend of Margaret's father's generation; also, a close friend had provided me with tales from their early school-days. Later, on my return to London, I was able to meet a former teacher of Margaret, who had been the only formidable opponent of her independent behaviour.

From these accounts emerged an intriguing picture of three generations of Leung women and men who embodied in their characters and background, in their relationships and activities, illuminating structures of domination and oppression, of public authority and the challenge to it by women's illicit powers. The history of three generations also makes plain the importance of historical treatment, the changes which affected women and which were effected by them. Over four long interviews (at times extending to five hours) Margaret told me about her grandmother, who had been a mooi-jai; about her mother, a daai-poh, who had been traditionally raised and came from a respectable family; about the concubine, a former prostitute, who ousted her mother from the rightful position of a daai-poh. She also talked about herself. She gave voice to the influence that mattered to her, she provided me with an insight into the life of a daughter who – wanting strength in others with which to identify – found it, not among men, but among the women of her family.

Her grandmother, Zhu Mei-rong, was born during the early 1880s, the same generation as Moot Xiao-li. Her father (Margaret's great-grandfather) was a poor hawker in a village not far from Guangzhou. His wife had died after giving birth to their first child, a daughter. When Zhu Mei-rong's father was out hawking his goods, women from the neighbourhood would keep an eye on his daughter. She was spirited and noisy for a girl and to keep her quiet, stories and legends about popular heroes and heroines were told her. The heroine who impressed herself most on the girl's mind was the courageous and independent female warrior Mu-lan.[56] The girl, too, wanted to do something for her father and make something of her life.

By all accounts Zhu Mei-rong must have been as different from the stereotypical image of submissive girlhood as is possible. Margaret's portrayal of her grandmother, whom she admired deeply, is no doubt idealized, but this portrait is partly verified by the subsequent life of Zhu Mei-rong.

She cleaned the hut, cooked the meals for her father as soon as she was old enough, and put a great deal of thought into plans for her future. Her father loved her; she may have been only a girl, but she was his only child and he was proud of her.

At the age of seven she asked her father whether he wanted to remarry. But even had he wanted to, he was so poor that even a widow – cheaper than a virgin – was outside his reach. She pleaded with him to sell her as a mooi-jai to a Guangzhou family. This is not as far-fetched as it may seem. The girl, impressed by Mu-lan's deeds, no doubt wanted to make her filial contribution to the father's face; only in this case there was no need for a warrior, but for money. The only way a girl of her age and station could make this money was by being sold. This payment to her father would enable him to remarry and do his duty by his ancestors.

There was another thought on the girl's mind, so the grandmother later told her favourite grand-daughter: as an only child, and despite her father being poor, he had spoilt her and she was loath to do physical work of the kind poor women in her village were wont to do. She observed them toiling in the fields and at home, suffering from the strains of frequent pregnancies, putting up with their husband's moods and beatings, labouring under dissatisfied and harsh mothers-in-law. She did not want such a fate.

Her father refused to sell her; but she kept on pressing him to contact a go-between. The next few years only hardened her resolve to let herself be sold and, if possible, to make her fortune (being clever and beautiful) among the rich. The life of a wife and daughter-in-law in an impoverished peasant family was not for her. She told Margaret how, after all the years which had passed since leaving the village, she still had visions of women transporting heavy loads, with babies strapped to their backs, walking in the heat of a humid summer day, sand rubbing the skin between their toes in open, peasant sandals.

When she was 14 years old her father gave in and asked a go-between to make enquiries in Guangzhou to see whether a wealthy family there might be in need of a mooi-jai. She was sold during the late 1890s and left her native village never to return; she was determined to help her father in any way she could.

The Purchasers and the Mooi-jai

Zhu Mei-rong was lucky; she was sold to a family where the daai-poh, a cultured and educated woman, needed a personal servant. This meant that she was able to enter into a close relationship with a woman who seemingly

CHART 6
Margaret Leung's family

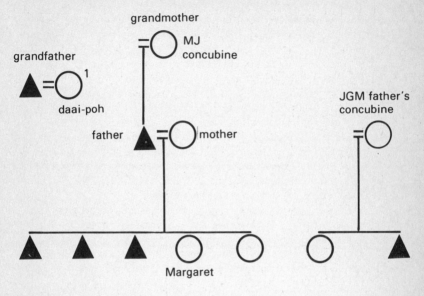

grandmother

grandfather

MJ
concubine

daai-poh

JGM father's
concubine

father

mother

Margaret

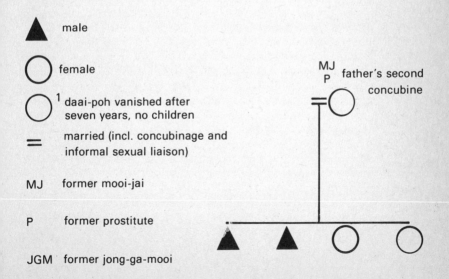

male

female

¹ daai-poh vanished after
seven years, no children

= married (incl. concubinage and
informal sexual liaison)

MJ former mooi-jai

P former prostitute

JGM former jong-ga-mooi

MJ
P father's second
concubine

treated her servants in a considerate manner. The master of the house was an official and for most of the time away on travels, accompanied by the first concubine. The daai-poh stayed at home to manage the large household and care for her mother-in-law. What the mooi-jai saw and heard in that household, what she observed by serving the daai-poh constituted an important part of her education.

Although the social distance between mistress and mooi-jai was never in question, the mooi-jai liked her comparatively comfortable life. But during all this time she never forgot her plans for the future. She adopted the mistress as a model of behaviour, which she would later utilize as a mistress of an even larger and more prominent household.

The mooi-jai kept her distance from the other servants and they never interfered with her. The mistress could be strict and they feared incurring her displeasure should she hear of discrimination against the mooi-jai. She was the only mooi-jai in that household, the rest were paid servants (amahs) who often cultivated an attitude of pride and arrogance towards mooi-jai, who were part of the master's property.

Tempers among the servants would flare up easily because of sexual rivalries between couples. Some amahs, having sworn themselves to a life of independence and spinsterhood, contracted lesbian relationships which were subject to strict codes of commitment and loyalty. In that particular household an especially temperamental couple of women would constantly break into violent quarrels as one suspected the other of infidelity with a young woman servant. Sometimes the servants' quarters were in a state of alarm at the passions aroused by a stray glance in the wrong direction, and one couple of amahs had to be dismissed when their domestic strife spilled over into the mistress's rooms.

The mooi-jai kept out of these quarrels and remained close to her mistress. Her tasks were light, and physical exertion was confined to fanning, striking matches, and filling the water-pipe. In the two years she worked in that household she grew to be very pretty and the mistress liked her presence.

One day the master of the house returned from an official visit to Hong Kong, bringing with him an old acquaintance whose wife had vanished recently – and who at that time had not been traced. The acquaintance, of the name of Leung, counted as one of the wealthiest Chinese in Hong Kong, a contractor whose good relations with the colonial government had brought him a vast fortune. When the wife welcomed the visitor her mooi-jai – then about 16 years old – was in attendance. She had served under a good mistress, but she was still a slave and outside the magic circle of wives and concubines.

However strong one's relationship with a woman from a higher class, as strong as the mooi-jai's relationship was with her mistress, that mistress was herself powerless when it came to the dominant world of men: men who controlled the sources of economic, political and social power and granted women access to them only through the channels of private relationships, defined by procreation and sexual gratification.

The young mooi-jai willingly became the concubine of the contractor Leung.

Rivalries and Survival

Exploring the friction between those women who, within their world, were accepted members and those who came from the 'outside', carrying with them the stigma of low face, it is interesting to observe the difference made by a time-span of 40 years. Around 1900 Margaret Leung's grandmother became the wealthy Hong Kong contractor Leung's concubine; during the late 1930s Margaret's mother was deposed from the position at her husband's side by another outsider, a former mooi-jai. The two situations were different, so were the characters of the women involved, but changes had taken place in attitudes towards marriage and family life that were at least as important. Whatever else changed in those 40 years, however, Chinese women in the 19th century, and in the 1930s, and still today, fought other women by male proxy.[57]

On the other hand, opportunities could be utilized in the 1930s by the concubine who defeated Margaret's mother, as they could not be utilized by Meng Achoi's concubine, Xiao-li, in 1912, when Xiao-li lost a decisive legal battle over the execution of Meng Achoi's testament. Both women influenced their husbands' testaments in their own favour and that of their descendants, and both were made executrix of the wills. But Xiao-li was handicapped by illiteracy and naivety in business matters and had to rely on lawyers and court-clerks who were more interested in self-enrichment than in winning her case. In the 1930s, women in general, particularly urban women, had greater opportunity for access to learning; not only learning in the formal sense, but in the sense of acquiring sophistication about the 'public world', that made this particular concubine, Margaret's mother's rival, so much more aware of social controls over women,[58] as she proved in her handling of the daai-poh's family. She was still subject to the same social and cultural controls that had bound Xiao-li, but the range of tactics she could employ to oppose these controls had increased.

Margaret's grandfather, of Mongolian stock, was an autocratic man, whose wealth had strengthened latent disciplinarian and abrasive characteristics in his personality. Progressive in his business dealings and life outside the home, when it came to governing domestic affairs he inclined towards traditional ways. He had been educated at one of the missionary colleges in Hong Kong and this educational influence mixed uneasily with his Chinese upbringing and mentality.[59]

His daai-poh stemmed from a staunchly Confucianist family and had been nurtured on the orthodox precepts of virtuous female behaviour as prescribed by Ban Zhao.[60] Her husband was so fond of her that even her childlessness did not upset the relationship, and he refused to let her go. She pleaded with him to take a concubine so that heirs might be born; he was the only surviving Leung. A devout Buddhist, his daai-poh considered her barrenness a sin for which she must atone by pressing for the purchase of a potential rival, but her husband 'refused to look at another woman'.[61] After seven years of childless marriage she ran away, thus presenting him with a *fait accompli* and obliging him to acquire a concubine.

A few months after his wife's disappearance, he saw the young and pretty mooi-jai, Zhu Mei-rong, in Guangzhou and took her as his concubine. Although the concubine never became a tin-fong, she was contented. She had no rival for the master's favours and her powerful position was assured. No sooner had she settled down than she sent a large sum of money to her father who bought land, a business, and a young wife. He was fortunate in enjoying the birth of several children, among them two sons. His face was saved, and he received respect and recognition from his neighbours.

The concubine acquired wealth and power in her home: in relation to the outside she was invisible. She did not crave for life beyond the courtyard. The household was governed in a feudal and patriarchal manner, and she helped to keep it that way. Herself a strong and determined woman, she upheld traditional notions on family life, on relations between the sexes and generations. When later the husband took seven more concubines, her domineering personality ruled them all and she never lost her monopoly over financial matters.[62]

She managed her only son and future heir to the estate with a love that made up for her own motherless childhood and years of deprivation. Apart from herself, numerous servants were at his beck and call; all these women made him the centre of a female-dominated universe. His father treated him coldly, from the emotional and physical distance demanded by his rank, but the care and affection lavished on the son by the women of his household amply compensated for the fatherly austerity. At the age of twelve, his father introduced him to a popular brothel in Hong Kong and he experienced his first sexual encounter with a highly-paid prostitute.

From then on these brothels became his favourite hunting grounds. Paternal restrictions grew irksome and at the age of 16 he left school to build up his own business at a time when much profit could be made in Hong Kong from land reclamation. By the age of 29 he had made his fortune and retired to spend the rest of his life pursuing his pleasures in the company of women. This pursuit had in no way been interfered with by his acceptance of an arranged marriage with a respectable young daughter (Margaret's mother) of a landed family in Guangdong.

Their first daughter, Margaret, now in her late 40s, told me a great deal about her late parents. Much of what she told me about them and her home reflected her own subjective dilemma in coming to terms with a strong personal identity in a world still essentially defined by men. Margaret's preoccupations with her father were obsessive and her assessment of him slightly ambivalent. On the one hand she regarded him as a strong and powerful male figure who moved in the public world unencumbered by restrictions suffered by women – making money, entertaining on a royal scale, enacting the eccentric habits of the very rich.[63] On the other hand, a strong and complex love-hate relationship with her unfortunate mother, who was 'cheated' by a 'low woman', made her contemptuous of her father's womanizing weakness.

Early childhood had made her idealize the father and loathe the weakness and passivity of her mother, a simple and bigoted woman. Her father, a sophisticated urbanite and *bon viveur*, was her model hero. Margaret received the first revelatory shock when her mother was pregnant again. Before the child was born the father moved out to join his new (and second) concubine, of whose existence his daai-poh had not been informed. The second key event in Margaret's relationship with her father came when she was 16 years old and accompanied him to a restaurant. He was surrounded by 'cheap and money-hungry vampires' and handed out $100 bills to every waitress present; when she saw 'how he stooped so low, not discriminating between good and bad women', she 'lost all respect for him'. She felt she had lost her father.

Margaret's life was overshadowed by 'that woman', the father's second concubine (with whom he lived in an establishment separate from the rest of the family), from the time of early childhood when she imitated her father's ways – to the extent of keeping up with his heavy drinking-habits – to the later period when each parent used her as a pawn to hurt the other. No one could control the girl who, although materially well-off, was emotionally deprived.

The second concubine, Lin Fang, a former prostitute, had initially been a mooi-jai to a prostitute in a brothel, and at the age of 13 was sold by her owner to another brothel. There she received basic education in reading and writing, singing and conversation, in order to attract rich clients. She had worked for several years before being taken as a concubine by Margaret's father. He bought her although she was already pregnant by another man; Margaret's father adopted the child but it died young from the effects of the mother's syphilis.

Lin Fang was clever and shrewd – to judge from the subsequent influence she had over the Leung family; she even sold the two children of the first concubine – who was by then dead – without opposition. She established herself in a different part of Hong Kong and was joined there by Margaret's father; he never returned to his first wife and her children. All ideological precepts and social conventions of a patrilineal society failed to enforce the daai-poh's rights and her sons' claims on the father's possessions.

With the physical proximity to her husband and his separation from the family, Lin Fang had accomplished an important tactical move; she had, *de facto*, substituted herself and her children for the family of Leung. Not only that, she spread the rumour that Margaret's mother was the low-class concubine and she herself the rightful daai-poh. Lin Fang was also much more versed in the conduct of financial business; she knew how to insure herself against future hardships. The father would 'load his children with money', handing it out freely to make up for his absence from the family home. But while the second concubine Lin Fang invested the money for her children in land and property, Margaret's mother regarded the money as potentially a bad influence on the children. She spent it on presents and outings so as to use it up immediately. What she did not suspect was that the substantial property holdings of her husband had gradually been changed over from his name to that of the concubine's. This was discovered only after the husband's death when the terms of the will were released.

Margaret's mother had always been very resentful towards her eldest daughter whose wild and unruly conduct reminded her of the estranged husband. The only person Margaret related to and could talk to about the father's hated mistress was that other former mooi-jai, her grandmother, Zhu Mei-rong. 'My grandmother,' Margaret said, 'was a political person in the sense that she could help herself and make her fortune despite her poor background. So she sold herself as a mooi-jai and became strong, she was clever and made positive decisions in her life.'

Despite the fact that Margaret's mother came from a younger generation, because of her background she was more deeply trapped in feudal thinking about the position of women. The fact that her feet had not been bound and that she had received a few years of formal education did not change her ingrained traditionalism; she was unable to make use of the opportunities that existed, her attitude towards life was marked by passivity.

Margaret told me that 'I always wanted to be strong and independent like my father, that is why I hated my mother. But when I was young I was sandwiched between pressure from above (the old influence) and from below (the young spirit).' Life spent in transition between the old and new made Margaret regretfully aware of customary constraints and missed opportunities.

While Margaret saw in her grandmother the independent 'political spirit' taking on life as a challenge, and in her mother the embodiment of passive female suffering – and making her children suffer for her bad fortune – Lin Fang, the second concubine, was seen as evil incarnate, destroying the beloved father and her own happy childhood. The personal involvement with these women and the understandable bias Margaret brought to her reminiscences blinded her to the fact that the grandmother and the 'evil' concubine shared the same features of low background and spirited challenge to its limitations. What was admirable about the grandmother, Margaret loathed in Lin Fang. Margaret had suffered defeat as a member of the daai-poh's family and viewed the concubine as a hated outsider.

The mother had confronted a woman who possessed the knowledge of a 'public' person, a self-confidence and deliberation which had their antecedence in the history of the grandmother.

The Grandmother and the Father's Concubine

In the spirit of her great model Mu-lan, Margaret's grandmother, Zhu Mei-rong, had saved her father's honour. She had helped him achieve his ambitions of raising a family and establishing a prosperous business. Although she never again visited him – her station in life had become too remote from his – the welfare of her parents' family was always to remain a major concern.

The Leung family offers yet another illustration of opposed loyalties, to the natal and conjugal families respectively: that of the concubine who outwitted Margaret's mother in the struggle for access to the head of the household. I have already told how she established herself in a common household with Margaret's father and over the years succeeded in changing the testament in favour of her children. According to my – admittedly biased – informant, the father's change of heart was not entirely due to the beauty and graces of his concubine Lin Fang, but to the pressures put upon him by her family.[64] Although it is not known how her brother approached Margaret's father in the first place, he assumed growing influence over him. By all accounts, this brother was an unsavoury character and a member of a Hong Kong gang which specialized in prostitution, gambling and blackmail. Probably, therefore, the father might have been the victim of some form of blackmail. Only once, when Margaret was already a grown-up woman, did he make a remark which suggested pressure from organized elements and his own vulnerability in the face of it.

Like the merchant To's wife, Margaret's mother had no link with her natal family. Unlike the wife of To, however, she had several sons. Evidence suggests that this fact, however crucial in theory in a patrilineal and patrilocal society, made no difference to the eventual outcome of the conflict between concubine and wife. Moral obligations (male) faltered in the face of (female) de facto power. The wife and her sons were weak, unable to push their rightful claims; the concubine not only stood in a uniquely close relationship to Margaret's father but also used her natal connections for the advancement of her children's future. The threat to Margaret's mother had come not from the claims of patriliny but from the rival claims of a uterine grouping within the same family.

I have already set out the story of Margaret Leung's grandmother. A generation later another mooi-jai became the concubine of a member of the Leung family. But important differences existed between the two women. It had not been in the interest of Margaret's grandmother to prejudice the future of her own children by the contractor Leung; she assisted her father but did nothing to endanger the Leung family's financial position.

The concubine Lin Fang acted quite differently. She established herself in a household, not only separate from, but opposed to that of the main branch, which already had a family of sons and daughters. It was in her interest and that of her family to divert the fortune away from the wife's family. In this she succeeded almost to the point of the latter's financial extinction.

To understand how such a situation could arise one needs to look at the personality of the man at the centre, Margaret's father. I came away from the interviews with an overwhelming impression of the superior strength of Chinese women; a strength that manifested itself particularly in their emotional hold over husbands and sons. A representative case was that of an old woman I used to visit in hospital. She was in her mid-90s and came from a well-to-do background. Her mother had been only the fourth concubine to a wealthy man in Hong Kong, but she proved herself so indispensable to the master and so powerful over the other women, that ultimately she controlled the purse-strings. The daughter profited from her mother's superior position and was given in marriage, as a tin-fong, to a young man of good family from the mainland. He later became the Chinese ambassador to a Latin-American country. The first wife had given birth to 'only' a daughter, thus the tin-fong's son was born into a household eagerly welcoming his arrival.[65] He was spoilt by his mother who sought to establish a lasting emotional hold over her son; she perhaps could not anticipate that by binding him to her she might be weakening him, with fatal consequences not only to her son. No restrictions were placed on the son's demands. When he went out, a servant followed him; whatever he chose to pick up, because it caught his fancy, was paid for by the servant who carried a large purse.[66] His mother treated him as a precious object, to be sheltered from the roughness of reality. Under her tutelage he never learned how to become an independent individual.

At 40 years old, he was unable to keep a steady job. As long as his mother is alive, her connections will help him out, with money and jobs. Incapable of forming relationships with women 'he has a woman every night'. He spends his money on them and on high living. A slave to his own fancies he is still the immature person he was in his amah's arms. His mother still supports him and stays at cheap hospitals to 'save his money'. His sister, too, accepts her brother's right to selfishly squander the money without a thought for his mother and sister's relatively impoverished circumstances. He is the head of the family despite the fact that he is incapable of directing even his own life. In and out of mental hospital, he is still the irresponsible and helpless boy his mother loves, his weakness being her strength.[67]

Margaret's father also was the centre of his mother's 'uterine family' – weak and dissolute – brought up in dependence on the women around him. But these mothers negated the very basis for their own future security by refusing to sever the umbilical cord. In Margery Wolf's Taiwanese families, the strong social order would have exerted the necessary social sanctions to make a man fulfil his familial obligations – whatever his proclivities and extra-family affairs.[68] This, however, was not the case in Hong Kong.

Self-regard and egocentricity had come to replace social responsibility and any sense of filial duty. In the upper-class élite, of which Leung was a member, the opportunities to show off wealth and consequence were great, and so was the temptation to outdo one's peers in ostentatious display. For Margaret's father the sense of duty towards his family was more than offset by the pleasure and company to be got from women who knew how to please, to flatter a man's susceptible ego, and how to follow up their advantage. Even when Margaret's father still lived at home, he was rarely present at family occasions.

Margaret's mother was the undisputed daai-poh and mistress of her home. The first concubine, once her jong-ga-mooi, was so submissive in her disposition that she constituted no threat. But what was the value of her undisputed control when the fount of power, vested in the head of the household, namely her husband, was removed from her domestic territory? She was paralysed. This paralysis transmitted itself to her children.

As we have noted, her mother was pregnant when Margaret first heard rumours that her father had set up a separate establishment with a woman of questionable credentials. Her offensive reputation was due not so much to the fact that she had worked as a prostitute and was pregnant by another man when the father bought her out, but that she had been a slave, a mooi-jai. It was this aspect of sale that placed Lin Fang outside the boundaries of common decency, more so than a prostitute who voluntarily or for filial reasons entered the profession. For Margaret – she was seven years old when the father left them – mooi-jai became a term loaded with evil, and loathsome attributes. She wanted 'to take a gun and shoot that woman'. The mother, stern and withdrawn by nature, made her daughter the scapegoat for her unhappiness because she resembled the estranged husband.

Margaret was, as she told me, 'wild with pain'. The beloved father had gone, discarding her in favour of an uncouth and vulgar woman. She blamed her mother for failing to keep him. Her witnessing of her mother's pain expressed itself in rebellious acts of defiance against the family's authority. Like many daughters from large and wealthy families, Margaret was raised by amahs. She controlled these with her violent temper and fits of rage, and they trembled with fear. The turn-over of amahs, not surprisingly, was large, because Margaret was such an unpredictable and exacting mistress. Yet she was kind too; in a generous moment she would give all her pocket-money to the amahs so that they could enjoy a meal at their favourite restaurant. Like her father, Margaret regarded money as the most effective means to acquire large numbers of friends and companions, and to keep them happy and in high spirits they were lavishly entertained.

So Margaret grew up undisciplined and wild, longing for the father and yet resenting what she came to see as his weakness and vanity. She loathed her mother's muted personality and evaded the motherly influence that had made her older brothers become as 'spineless' as their father. But lacking the charm and sharp business-sense of their father, they never got as far in their lives. Margaret speaks of them with contempt.

Loneliness seemed to have been the most predominant feature in her life.

Only one instance can she remember when her mother came close to caress her. When I asked her about the relationship with her amah she only replied, 'she was paid to do it'. Margaret changed schools more often than she can remember. If she did not like a teacher or objected to the discipline she told her amah to register her at another school. One of her former school-fellows remembers the terrible tantrums, the swooning whenever Margaret wanted to create a scene, the fits of hysterics. More and more she created for herself a reality of romantic events with herself at the centre. She finally ended up at a Convent school; but this seemed to have had little impact on her behaviour. From an early age she signed her own school reports. Her mother could not read English, her father was not accessible, her brothers refused to sign the reports, because she was referred to, and condemned, as a rebellious pupil. She was a heroine among her classmates, so she said. This must have reinforced her self-image of the feckless fighter against social restraints and familial oppression.

When she was 14 years of age, she refused to attend school and was persuaded to change her mind only when her father offered her a salary and asked her to look on it as a job; which she did. When the teachers reprimanded her she would say, 'I am paid to be here'. These early experiences of her mother's weakness in the face of a strong and anarchic outsider and rival, of the father's vanity and dependence on women to prop up his ego, of her observations in the large feudal household, combined with her own position of unfettered independence, are important in understanding some of the formative pressures on Margaret's personality. Conflicting models of womanhood resulted in the adoption of neither. The parental *carte blanche* given to her upbringing made her miss the boundaries of emotional security, but also granted her a unique opportunity for the evasion of oppressive conventions and for detached observation of Chinese society in operation.

For Margaret no authority figure existed. Everyone, from mother, father, to grandmother and amahs, could be, and was, resisted. Margaret was fearless because no one invested in her emotionally. She had nothing to lose and she was 'free' and, therefore, reckless. The only two persons who meant something to her were physically and emotionally removed (her father) or had passed away early in her childhood (her paternal grandmother).

As a child she was called the 'crying bun' – she wept much because she mourned her father. But in her teens, the tough and strong image of the warrior-heroine took over. She decided not to be lured by money prospects into obedience, as had happened with her sisters and brothers.

When I realized I would get no inheritance as a daughter I did what I wanted to do. If I was good I would not get anything. If I was bad I still would not get anything, so I could not lose out. Some daughters, of course, wanted a good dowry and so they were obedient. But I thought I would marry a rich man, so I didn't need a dowry. And in any case, if I did marry a rich man my family would not want to lose face and give me the dowry anyway.

A good deal of commonsense and cynical observation combined to produce these remarks. As she told me, everyone in her household, like everyone else in Hong Kong, crawled before money. The lives of all her friends were determined by the hope of some future financial windfall.

Women, from her point of observation, were even more vulnerable. Before they married they had to obey their families, after their marriage they had to obey their husband's family. Why get married at all? she would ask herself. Why should she give up the precious independence which a husband would be bound to take away from her? Thus she scandalized her mother and relations by refusing all hands in marriage. As a friend of Margaret told me, because of her escapades many families were reluctant to take in such a wilful daughter-in-law. The only inducement being a large dowry, it came as no surprise to the friend that Margaret's indifference to a dowry, publicly pronounced, further discouraged these families.

A spirit of fierce independence made her despise the pressures of public opinion so vital as an operative agent in Chinese society. She feels, so she often told me, that the conventionalism of Chinese women in her class is largely the result of this public pressure that stifled their ability to look beyond the narrow confines of the domestic well. As an illustration of the terrible impotence felt by Chinese women, Margaret referred to the high suicide rate in Hong Kong. Her comment was: 'Why do these women not envisage an alternative life-style and go and make their own lives instead of conceding defeat in such a terrible way? But I can understand that they want to make an end to a life of serving and more serving... who can continue this sort of existence?'[69] But she also conceded that for many, if not most women in Hong Kong, there was little alternative, as they were economically dependent on their husbands. She had been able to take advantage of opportunities available to women today because of her class background and the material security that gave her.

With great pride she referred to the independence of the women of Shunde. The lives of these women were well-known to women outside this 'notorious' district of Guangdong.[70] Many women of the older generation whom I met in Hong Kong remembered the women of Shunde without prompting on my part: the pilot-history of female independence held alive by women in the southern parts of China. Margaret's family had employed several amahs from the Shunde district and they had told her much about life in their villages. Shunde constituted as much an important part of women's consciousness as the knowledge of the frequent occurrence of female infanticide in Guangdong and Fujian before liberation. 'Shunde' and 'female infanticide' constituted two opposites in a continuum of female life in traditional Chinese society. Neither may have come within the realm of experience of a particular woman, but they were no less potent in influencing her subjective identification of femaleness, that of which she was a part.

When Margaret was 16 years old she made her dramatic bid to join the revolution on the mainland. This was in 1949. Guangzhou's outlying areas saw the struggles of peasants against landlords in the wake of the liberation. In Hong Kong Margaret followed events with intense commitment and impulsively decided to become part of the revolution. For that purpose she bought a white horse and suitable garments to show off a heroine committed to 'fight to the bloody end'. Dressed in white, seated on a white horse, she felt that she could not fail to create the kind of historical impact she craved to make. The garments had been bought, the horse stabled, but Margaret experienced unexpected difficulties from her family. The mother threatened to kill herself, the brothers threatened to keep her back forcibly; friends were alerted and asked for advice, but it seemed nothing could break the determination of the young girl. In the end her father was informed, and proved himself the only one not to recoil in horror at the prospects of revolution in the family. He asked her to reflect on it and give herself a fortnight. This she consented to do. As this fortnight was filled with social engagements with her father she forgot her personal deadline and the horse remained stabled. The events of that year are now referred to as 'the Guangzhou epic' – a friend of Margaret's father told me that she could now understand the young girl's craziness: retaliation against the world that had not wanted her; the struggle in China was seen by Margaret as part of her own personal struggle.

Margaret is now in her late 40s. Still unusual for a Chinese woman in Hong Kong she has chosen to remain single and to keep a lover when and if it suits her. Her family is scandalized but helpless, as she lives in her own flat on her own private income. Margaret is wise and candid about much which concerns female inequality and social conventions in Chinese circles. But she herself has not quite escaped. Disorientated and insecure she has turned day into night, and night into day, choosing to spend her waking hours in night-clubs and restaurants where she is as well-known as her father once was. There I accompanied her for the interviews and there she told me about the family's and, by implication, her own personal history.

She had spent several years of her youth at convent schools, where she encountered the Christian concepts of evil and good. She could never accept the total damnation of Lucifer – hell to her was different: it was here on this earth that we created hell for ourselves. She herself went through hell in her childhood, and is still overcome by sadness so that her only relief is in 'creating heaven for others'. Her limitless generosity stems from this.

There were other implications for Margaret. The right of all people 'to benefit from heaven' was the right that all people had equal standing. Certainly this is no Confucianist notion. This emphasis on equality was an assertion on her part that women in Chinese society had their rights; in her own, if eccentric, life-style, she had tried to realize this ambition.

But more crucial than such an abstract concept was the concrete intervention of two outsider women in the history of the Leung family, and, therefore, in the life of Margaret Leung. However different in their impact on the family's fortunes, their low-class origins and slave-status moulded their characters outside the female stereotype for upper-class women. In turn their characters propelled their fates from slavery to wealth and power. In their transcendence of social boundaries they provided Margaret with models to which she responded with love and admiration, with hate and bitterness. The circumstances of her birth made the nature of rebellion one from within the family, but a challenge to the family structure nevertheless.

To understand her way of life as it developed is to be conscious of the part played by two women in her family who also 'did not know their place'.

Reflections

These biographies have traced slavery and post-slavery – from mooi-jai to concubine status from the 'inside', the domestic world of women: that is, the slaves were seen in relation to the group of women who, in their allocated social roles, mirrored the patriarchal preoccupations of society, to do with exchange and procreation. When patriarchal evaluation and economic disparity forced females into slavery, it also positioned them outside the socially validating chain of reproduction and the sole source of security for women: the nurturing of uterine ties. Slavery was life in the margin, in conditions of exploitation and social vulnerability which grew more oppressive for the mooi-jai as the contradiction grew between new notions of sexual equality permeating Hong Kong society, and patriarchal resistance to it – helped by the absence of economic alternatives for single women.

The termination of the mooi-jai status, when it occurred, was not automatically succeeded by a full integration of the former mooi-jai into the rank of free women. The more far-reaching her upward-mobility, the heavier the legacy of her past was encumbered with prejudices and reservations. The fear of her was the fear of her former ambiguous status; the fear of the corruptive influences associated with the polluting 'baseness' of her mooi-jai existence. She could never be trusted to have internalized proper models of behaviour and, like the notorious Imperial concubines of the past, she was prone to abuse power, to violate boundaries that existed to protect society from chaos. This was the fear which had made Old To such a potent figure. The threat was to male-dominated values, but no less to woman-centred uterine units whose existence and survival were dependent on the former.

Margery Wolf suggested the concept of 'uterine family' to encompass the mother-centred ties, ties which, because of their emotional potency, could give rise to the exercise of power by women over their sons' households.[71]

The biographies of outsider-women such as Moot Xiao-li, To's Xiang

Fei, and Leung's concubine, illustrate their means of acquisition of power, namely sex. 'Illicit' means offered the only opportunity to gain direct access to a male, their husband, by-passing those women higher in orthodox ranking and public consideration – and upsetting all expectations about patrilineal succession.

The threat to the economic survival of one woman's 'uterine group' in a polygamous household derived from another woman's vested interests in the survival of her own uterine group (Meng and Leung families) or from a more selfish motivation (Old To). The conflict was between women in a culture where women were powerful through men, but by themselves enjoying no access to authority. Outsiders were feared and the former mooi-jai would always be mistrusted. While the expectations for Chinese men in Hong Kong were to rise in fortune, wealth and status, and to move upwards into a higher social class, women were given their place in society by men and expected to do justice to it by proper conduct.[72]

Among themselves, women inside the women's community acted differently; in relation to men they were 'muted', in their own spheres other codes of behaviour applied.[73] The marginal woman, detached from either paradigm, that of the male and the female worlds within orthodox kinship, could develop character-traits that exploited the male view, that women (for example, mooi-jai) were no threat, by turning the physical proximity within a household into an invitation to greater intimacy – the intimacy of sex constituting her sole avenue to power.

Analysing the components of the phenomenon of mooi-jai within the context of individual mooi-jais' biographies, different emphases and behaviour-patterns emerge, which sometimes coincide with that of public structures. More often, however, they diverge to constitute their own logical patterns in a realm where women have to deal with other women through men. Here women occupy the main-stage of action, so to speak, and men become peripheral actors while, as symbols, retaining the capacity of authority-givers. Here it is men who act as symbols. In the same way as 'outside' (in the public world) men use women to enhance their prestige or manly self-esteem; viewed from the 'inside' the reverse is the case.

The exploitative nature of slavery is ever-present, but by viewing it through the eyes of individual women I have shown their potential ability to acknowledge the limitations they were subject to and to turn them to their advantage.

That women do not necessarily allow themselves to be browbeaten by fate into passive acquiescence, does not alter the fundamental fact of the injustice of this fate. Nor does it ever justify the waste of many lives which were lived powerlessly and helplessly subject to the whims of masters who peremptorily exercised control over what they regarded as their rightful property.

There are the shadowy statistics of innumerable slave-girls who always remained slaves and who ended their lives the way they had begun – as outsiders. In Hong Kong I encountered three such women.

4. Ma Xin's Mooi-jai, Yuet-Sim, Number Three Mooi

Ma Xin's mooi-jai, Yuet-Sim, and Number Three mooi remained with their owners beyond the stipulated age of marriage – only Ma Xin's mooi-jai eventually broke loose from the oppression that had destroyed her life.

Ma Xin's Mooi-jai

I never met Ma Xin's mooi-jai (that was how she was called, she was never given a name) because she had vanished in 1968. I interviewed Ma Xin at great length; she was very frank about the negotiations of 1948. I also interviewed a good woman friend of the mooi-jai, who is, however, as ignorant about her whereabouts as everyone else seems to be. The material I received from Ma Xin had to be carefully sifted; it nevertheless allowed a life-history of the mooi-jai and Ma Xin which is worth presenting for the attitudes it revealed and the information it gives on the uses to which women were put by other women.

The mooi-jai was born around 1931 – obviously it is impossible to be more precise. She grew up in a village in the vicinity of Guangzhou, and her parents worked the land of their landlord. When the girl was about eight years old the landlord called the father and told him that he was to be relieved of the obligations towards his young daughter; he should rather save the grain for his sons. The reason for the landlord's sudden interest in his tenant's daughter was the wedding of his own daughter, soon to take place. She was going to be married off to a neighbouring lineage and the father meant to raise her status with her parents-in-law by adding a jong-ga-mooi to her dowry.

It is not known how – if at all – he compensated the girl's parents but on the day the bride left her parents' home in the bridal sedan-chair, the jong-ga-mooi formed part of the display which traditionally accompanied the bride's wedding procession.

The jong-ga-mooi was never to see her natal family again.

Purchasers and Mistresses

Little is known about the girl's first mistress. All that emerged when the girl was sold a second time was that her young master had taken a fancy to her and provoked scenes of conjugal jealousy. The girl was in her teens and for all intents and purposes kept as a mooi-jai. More importantly, the mother-in-law of the young mistress did not approve of the prospect of a concubine for her son and took the girl sharply to task. The mooi-jai was accused of provocative behaviour and unseemly deportment. When the mother-in-law heard, through a go-between, that someone in Guangzhou was prepared to pay a good price for a mature mooi-jai, they declared their willingness to sell the girl. The go-between arranged for the transfer and made out the deed of sale.

This second sale took place in 1948, in Guangzhou. The new purchaser, a woman, Ma Xin, who was prepared to pay such a high price came from Shanghai, where she had worked as a prostitute. In her early 30s she had been bought out by a goldsmith to be his wife; and so successful had she been in her profession, that with her savings the husband could start an independent business. They had been married for more than ten years; she was now 45 years old, and still no child had been born.

Ma Xin, a strong and determined person, dominated her husband. Shortly before removing themselves from Guangzhou in 1948, when the political situation became too uncertain for them and Hong Kong had been liberated from Japanese occupation, Ma Xin decided that she would have to buy a young girl to produce what she was unable to produce, namely heirs. Ma Xin told me that the requirements were for a young girl who would be subservient to her (she would tolerate no rival) and who had learned to obey – ideally a mooi-jai. For that she was prepared to pay a great deal. It also had to be a girl without kin, so that she would be able to take her with them to Hong Kong, without the girl's natal family interfering. The girl offered by the go-between was ideal. It was obvious to Ma Xin that the master and mistress were eager to get rid of the jong-ga-mooi and no questions asked. According to Ma Xin, the husband agreed to the scheme (his wife paid for it) and the girl was installed as a mooi-jai; her main function was to reproduce. She was never given the status of a concubine but remained a mooi-jai.

When the young girl was sold a second time she felt no sorrow at the thought of parting. 'It was all one to her' – said my informant. She, the jong-ga-mooi, was not told what her new proprietors expected from her, only to pack her belongings and accompany the go-between to Guangzhou. She never saw the mistress again.

Ma Xin and her husband took her to Hong Kong; they started a new jewellery business, which got off to a slow start – as no one ordered many jewels so soon after the deprivations of war and occupation. The mooi-jai had been bought at the age of 17 and remained there for about 20 years; she ran away in 1968. The family first lived in a make-shift hut, but

CHART 7

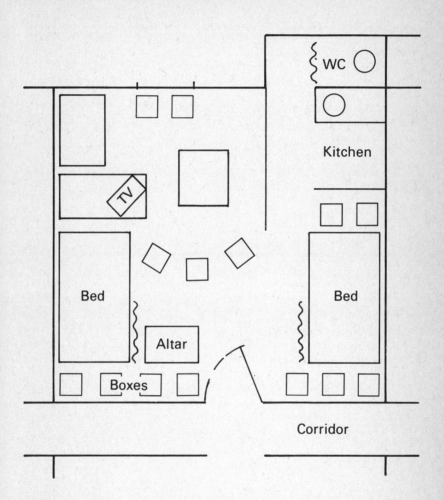

Ma Xin's home

The room Ma Xin's family and mooi-jai have lived in since shortly after their arrival from Guangzhou. The family still lives there and in that room I interviewed Ma Xin.

In 1978 six adults shared the overcrowded space: Ma Xin and her husband, two sons and their wives.

comparatively quickly managed to get a room on one of the resettlement estates in Hong Kong.

The mooi-jai cleaned the room, did the washing, shopped, served the wife and served her husband. She did her duty by giving birth to six children, four of them boys. They addressed her as a servant: the title of mother was reserved for Ma Xin. What the woman's feelings were can scarcely be imagined.

She rarely admitted her friend, my informant, to her inner world. My informant, a perceptive woman, said of her, 'it was as if she was never quite present' – a self-effacing and reserved woman about whom it was believed that she would never extricate herself from Ma Xin; a woman who even within the domestic world, the world of women, had no place of her own. To use E. Ardener's terminology, even within the sub-dominant structures where women made themselves heard on their own terms and established their own hierarchical order, she was 'mute'; a true outsider lacking the relational context by which she could have made herself heard, she had no access to status.[74] Known only as Ma Xin's mooi-jai, oppressed from an early age, when faced with dominance she submitted. Then she staged the only protest she was ever known to make – silently she withdrew, never to reappear. Ma Xin, boasting about the good bargain she struck in 1948, lamented the additional work for herself. 'What was wrong with her that she would run away, silly woman.'

Yuet-sim and Number Three Mooi

Yuet-sim was kidnapped when about three years old, she thinks; she remembers nothing about her natal family. She believes that she may have come from a village in the vicinity of Guangzhou, but this is only speculation. She does not talk about this, it still hurts and shames her. Most of the questions I wanted to ask her I had to ask through a trusted person. When I met her she mostly smiled and let others talk for her (by the time I met Yuet-sim I had made the acquaintance of several women she knew). It took a long time to arrange a meeting, as her master was unwilling to let her socialize with strangers. Her extreme shyness made it necessary to employ the good offices of others, who constituted a common meeting-ground for Yuet-sim and myself. An interpreter taken from outside her circle would have been disastrous under these circumstances.

Yuet-sim, then in her late 60s, still worked for the same family to whom she was sold, through a go-between, by the kidnappers. She thinks she may have been stolen by a gang of disbanded soldiers who then roamed the countryside of Guangdong and who had subsequently sold her in Hong Kong. So painful is the memory of that event, of which she is only half aware, that I was warned, prior to our encounter, not to be too insistent in my questioning.

Number Three mooi could barely remember the times when she was not in the household of the Lai family where she had served, first as a mooi-jai, and later as an amah. She comes from 'somewhere in Guangdong' and her parents were very poor. The father was an artisan who was mostly unemployed. He came from an insignificant lineage, the members of which were spread over different villages and even districts.

This man knew the aunt of a neighbour who worked as a servant in Hong Kong, and when the woman came to join her family during the New Year celebrations, he asked her whether her employer's family could take in one of his daughters, as he could not afford to keep her. The servant took father and daughter with her to Hong Kong and the father pleaded with the mistress of the household to accept the girl. After some thought this was done. The girl was two years old. The father returned to his home village and never again set eyes on her. The son of the then master of this wealthy family told me that they had already taken in two other mooi-jai and had no use really for such a small girl. But they took her in because 'they pitied her'.

The little girl was handed over to the amahs and the girl's father received some 'lucky money' to compensate for the expenses and pains of upbringing. In the case of wealthy families, the 'taking in' of a mooi-jai was seen as a charitable act and no sung-tip was drawn up. The girl was called Number Three (as the third mooi-jai). She was introduced to me as Number Three. The family had retained this form of address, although the 1923 Female Domestic Ordinance had legally changed her status to one of paid servant.

The Purchasers

Yuet-sim was sold to the large Yeo family. The master's father, a once successful and wealthy comprador and member of that exclusive 19th century Chinese élite, had consolidated his wealth and public standing by marrying a well-respected official's daughter from Guangzhou, and later by purchasing three concubines. The first two were prostitutes; the second prostitute had bought a mooi-jai before she met the comprador Yeo and she took the girl to her new home. In time the mooi-jai became concubine Number Three, but always remained a mooi-jai in relation to her former mistress.

Yuet-sim's master, son of the first concubine, only attained the post of a moderately successful clerk, unlike his father. His marriage to the daughter of a clerk (the son of a comprador from the same generation as Yeo senior) produced no issue and he bought a prostitute from Sham-shui-po (a notorious district in Hong Kong), who gave birth to four children. The financial standing of the family not being of the best, a mooi-jai (Yuet-sim) was acquired who was responsible for running the household and caring for the children.

Number Three mooi was an infant when taken into the master's family and naturally too young to serve. A woman servant from the large staff was instructed to care for the child. When Number Three had been in the Lai family for a few months she became seriously ill. The master's son, who was only a few years older than Number Three, told me that the mooi-jai was put into a home, the Italian Convent in Hong Kong, because there she could not infect the servants. The former mooi-jai herself did not comment on this episode in her life. The child remained at the Convent for two years and was then taken back by the Lai family. She was entrusted with the personal service of a young daughter of the master's family and remained with her until the mistress's death in 1968.

Yuet-sim worked hard and well and, being undemanding, she would have been contented – knowing no other life; but her mistress, the concubine, treated her harshly and contemptuously. Her existence was acknowledged only if services were required and then she had to tolerate ill-temper, coarseness and – when the mistress was in the mood – beatings. Yuet-sim herself never commented on the kind of household she had served for so long. It was left to her acquaintance (the informant who had introduced me to her) to elaborate on her tale with sharp and succinct comments. These observations boiled down to the claim that women from the 'outside' (the mistress, a former prostitute, had been purchased by the brothel-keeper, and raised by her) must be expected to behave in this cruel fashion.

'They had no education'; having no respectable mother to model themselves on, how could they be expected to grow into respectable women? Despite the recognition that role models were important in the process of social learning, the concubine was held guilty by my informant for her cruelty towards Yuet-sim, however strong the mitigating factors of environment and formative relationships.

The master did not interfere with household affairs ('he was too busy visiting prostitutes') and his wife did not concern herself with the unhappiness of a mere mooi-jai. As the first wife had bound feet, in contrast to the large-footed concubine, she seldom stirred from her room.

During this time of Yuet-sim's unhappiness, anti-mooi-jai agitation in Hong Kong had culminated in the 1923 Female Domestic Ordinance, and after years of inactivity, had produced a further strengthened Amendment to the Ordinance in 1929 (see Appendix A). The agitation, which involved extensive newspaper coverage and public campaigning, did not affect Yuet-sim's life. For all it was worth to her, the campaign might never have taken place. She neither heard about it nor did anyone tell her; whether her master and mistress knew or not, she could not say. For Yuet-sim the world was unchanging, the points of reference remained static. Mistress, children, other servants formed the constituent parts of her life and she could not imagine that her humble position in it might ever be called into question. If she was unhappy, then this unhappiness must be borne with patience and resignation.

In December 1929, in the wake of the Amendment, all mooi-jai owners were called upon to register their mooi-jai, pay regular wages and release them from their bonds at the age of 18 years. Yuet-sim was not too sure about her age, but she was at least 18 years at that time. Not that she knew about the law, but the master, working in government administration, was known to keep a mooi-jai, and for the sake of his office he felt obliged to act in accordance with the official policies. He might have married her off, or offered her paid employment in his own or some other household. But the loss of a loyal and hardworking drudge so angered the concubine that she ordered Yuet-sim out of the house.

In 1929 the Hong Kong Secretariat for Chinese Affairs (SCA) appointed Inspector Fraser and, in 1930, two Chinese women inspectors to supervise registered mooi-jai; one of them put Yuet-sim into the Po Leung Kuk, the Chinese home for the protection of women and girls, where she remained for several years.

Number Three mooi, like Yuet-sim, grew up in total ignorance of political and social events and the changes around her. She was a most loyal and faithful mooi-jai to her young mistress, and so identified with her joys and sorrows that everything else was shut out of her life. When I asked her about her personal history she told me the history of her late beloved mistress. It was as if she had disappeared into the persona of the mistress. There was no self.

She was contented with her life and did not mourn her natal home: she had never known it. Her close relationship with the young mistress ensured her of a position of respect among the servants of the house. In the same way that women generally depended for rank and status on their husbands, these mooi-jai were accorded courtesy or contempt by other servants in relation to their standing with a member of the master's family. This had no implication of kinship assimilation (the distance between the two classes from which mistress and mooi-jai came was far too great), but it showed an acknowledgement by servants that a mistress could extend considerable protection to a humble mooi-jai which singled her out from the rest of the household staff. It was a personal gesture and only in so far and so long an alleviation of the mooi-jai's condition as the mistress chose to make it.

Number Three mooi never heard of registration of mooi-jai, but with occasional money-gifts her status was subtly changed to that of an amah, and the Lai family was saved the loss of a valued servant, and from social embarrassment (concerted agitation had proclaimed mooi-jai to be slaves). Number Three mooi followed her mistress to the bridegroom's home and stayed with her until the latter's death. In 1968, having no other place to go, she returned to the Lai family, to serve as a domestic.

The Nature of Servitude

In the case of Ma-Xin's mooi-jai, her status was perceived both by the mooi-jai and her owner as valid for life. This life-sentence was terminated only because the mooi-jai ran away. For Yuet-sim and Number Three mooi, a change in their status amounted to nothing more than a nominal procedure that left the essence of their oppression untouched.

By contracting a specific alliance with a powerful man, those women discussed earlier were enabled to acquire a change in status. Through these men – in exchange for required services – such women could gain access to male recognition of an altered status, and to the material benefits accruing from the new status, for example, those due to a concubine. This channel of power was not open to women who served a household in a general, or their mistress in a personal capacity. Mistresses could relieve the conditions of work, and good mistresses could transmute drudgery into identity-giving vocations, but they could never grant the recognition which was essential to bring about the change from slavery to non-slavery. Those who granted that recognition had to be members of the dominant structures of society, namely men; thus the possibility of change in the status of female 'states' – in contrast to male slavery – says something too about the relationship between the two sexes: the power of men to decide the fates of women.

The fluidity in the status of female slaves – in contrast to that of male slaves[75] – was therefore symptomatic of women's generally low public status. A woman was nothing unless she was validated through kinship relations with a *male* – in the capacity of daughter, mother, wife, and so on.

This was the crucial structural distinction between the kinless state of a concubine whose relationship with a husband, however tentative, gave her a recognized function in society, and the kinless state of a slave who remained outside the community of women defined in terms of positions within a spectrum of kinship-dependence on men.

Not inhabiting publicly demarcated roles, the transmutations from one state to another in a woman's life took place in personalized ways – the condition of transmutation being the presence of an authoritative male and his intervention on behalf of a woman: her only way to social validation.

Ma Xin's mooi-jai, Yuet-sim, and Number Three mooi were never drawn into this circle of women with access to male authority. Their slave (outsider) status positioned them within the twilight penumbra of social life. Ma Xin used her mooi-jai's reproductive capacities for her own ends; in other words she appropriated her mooi-jai as an extension of herself, instrumental to the preservation of the social unit of which she and the husband were the two parties, to the exclusion of the mooi-jai. Here one cannot speak of a relationship between the man and the mooi-jai; the latter was used as proxy, and her status determined, by Ma Xin. The husband had no voice in this.

Yuet-sim had always been a mooi-jai in the service of the concubine. When she left the Po Leung Kuk, she returned to the family, having nowhere else to go and no natal family to return to. Soon after her return the first wife and the concubine died, but – for a pittance – Yuet-sim continued to work for the master and his family. After the children had left Hong Kong to go abroad, she stayed with the master in Hong Kong and still worked for him when I interviewed her. His fortunes and health had declined drastically and, no longer able to get about, he had retired. Yuet-sim nursed him, cooked, washed, shopped – and could not afford even to buy herself a pair of trousers.

The old man, though ill, still longed for female company, and having to make concessions to contemporary attitudes, he pondered the question of marriage. I was told that 50 years ago he would not have hesitated but resolved the problem by taking Yuet-sim as a mistress. Yuet-sim was not asked by her master, she was assumed to be willing. But the children, who supported their father financially, vetoed the marriage and threatened to cut him off should he carry out his intention. Their argument was that, even in 1978, a former mooi-jai would inevitably bring disgrace upon a family such as theirs. The fact that they were descended from a prostitute-concubine was studiously ignored. Yuet-sim was *still* associated with the mooi-jai status and that carried with it sufficient opprobrium to nullify recognition of her life-long services to the family and to a decrepit and stodgy octogenarian. She remained the outsider she was when mooi-jai existed as a social institution. This kind of past continues to feature in assessments of individual women in Hong Kong.

All her life Number Three mooi had been dependent on the master's family, and this dependence, along with her status as an essential outsider, continued without change even after a change had been legally brought about. After the mistress's death she went back to the household she had served as a mooi-jai and continued to work for the former master's son and his family. Her life did not change, but her length of service, intimate knowledge of the people she worked for, and the daily proximity, established for her a situation of mutual trust and warmth.

Seen objectively her status had altered little, if at all, from earlier days; but for Number Three mooi old age mellowed much of what was harsh and indifferent in the employers' attitude towards her. While still 'the other', she was the other in a small domestic world embracing both master and servant, known intimately to both and where each perceived the other to be an important and necessary, if unequal, partner, without whom it would be difficult to make sense of the world.

Part 2.   The Tapestry

5. Hong Kong Society: Positions, Perceptions and Attitudes[1]

The centre-stage has so far belonged to the individuals: Moot Xiao-li and her descendants, Margaret Leung's grandmother and the other women in her family, Old To, Ma Xin's mooi-jai, Yuet-sim, and Number Three mooi. But their individual fates can only be understood against the fate of others like them; the mooi-jai practice was a salient part of an era of the history of Chinese women which is still inscribed on the minds of its survivors and their descendants, and which marks the road that Chinese women have travelled since then.

Early despatches, covering the period from 1880 to 1882, between Hong Kong and the Colonial Office (CO) in London consistently denied the existence of slavery on British colonial territory, arguing that after all it had been outlawed since 1833.[2] And, indeed, this official position did continue for a long time to bedevil attempts at a realistic assessment of social conditions in the Colony. In China, too, slavery had been outlawed since the Qing Government issued a decree in 1910 prohibiting both public and private slavery.[3] But national and man-made calamities on the mainland had created conditions which exacerbated the customary practice of commercial trafficking in girls for the purposes of domestic drudgery and prostitution.[4] This gulf between legal and social reality was transferred to Hong Kong where the open border with Guangdong Province, and the Hong Kong Government's promise of toleration of Chinese customs, gave rise to a contradictory situation whereby the practice of slavery could exist for so long because in law it had ceased to exist.

Generally speaking, up to 1922, the CO took its cue from Hong Kong in terms of evaluation of local political sensitivity about the mooi-jai issue and in regard to policy decisions. The basic premise was, firstly, the mooi-jai custom constituted a long established tradition conceived as a charitable institution for the benefit of poor females (and as such likely to be misunderstood by European do-gooders); secondly, the alternative to the mooi-jai custom was either death by exposure or starvation, or sale into prostitution, for surplus female infants; and thirdly, the difficulty of

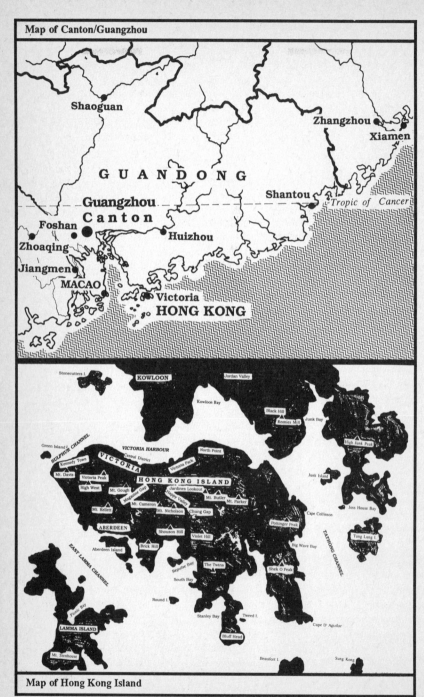

Map of Canton/Guangzhou

Shaoguan

Zhangzhou
Xiamen

G U A N D O N G

Shantou

Tropic of Cancer

Guangzhou
Canton

Foshan

Huizhou

Zhoaqing

Jiangmen

MACAO

Victoria
HONG KONG

Stonecutters I.

KOWLOON   Jordan Valley

Kowloon Bay

Black Hill
Rennies Mill   Junk Bay

Green Island I.   High Junk Peak

SULPHUR CHANNEL

VICTORIA HARBOUR

North Point

Kennedy Town   Central District

VICTORIA   Victoria Park

Mt. Davis

Victoria Peak   HONG KONG ISLAND   Junk Island

High West

Mt. Gough   Jardines Lookout

Magazine Gap   Mt. Butler

Mt. Cameron   Happy Valley   Mt. Parker

Mt. Kellett   Joss House Bay

Mt. Nicholson   Chung Gap

Cape Collinson

ABERDEEN   Pottinger Peak

Shouson Hill   Tung Lung I.

Aberdeen Island   Violet Hill

Brick Hill   Big Wave Bay

EAST LAMMA CHANNEL   TATHONG CHANNEL

Repulse Bay   The Twins

South Bay   Shek O Peak

Round I.

Picnic Bay

Stanley Bay   Tweed I.   Cape D' Aguilar

LAMMA ISLAND

Bluff Head

Mt. Stenhouse

Beaufort I.   Sung Kong

Map of Hong Kong Island

interfering with a longstanding Chinese custom was such that a realistic policy would seek the path of accommodation rather than (potentially dangerous) confrontation. The last point was closest to the hearts and minds of decision-makers in Hong Kong and London. As Hong Kong Governor Sir Reginald Stubbs put it in 1921, 'The Chinese will stand most things but will stand least of all interference with their family affairs. For that reason we interfere in these affairs as little as possible.'[5]

The CO's resistance to positive legislative actions on the mooi-jai issue was further reinforced by an influential memorandum, submitted by the Secretary for Chinese Affairs, E. R. Hallifax (in 1921), which did a great deal to shape perceptions in London; the memorandum was widely circulated in government circles in London and constituted the basis for subsequent CO publications and House of Commons statements.[6]

But domestic changes in Britain in the inter-War years had their effects on the course of colonial administration in Hong Kong. The growth of the Labour Party and increased social legislation contributing towards the establishment of a welfare state, were symptomatic of a change in the political climate which, as a result, rendered Hong Kong a pointedly conspicuous monument to unfettered private enterprise.[7]

Public pressure in Britain over the mooi-jai practice was largely a vote of disaffection from the Hong Kong administration, which continued to claim that Hong Kong must be exempted from the trend in Britain towards greater liberalization of government. It was effectively organized public action in Britain (initiated in 1919) and in Hong Kong that moved a recalcitrant Government in Hong Kong into legislative action – despite its continued worries about threats to the economic survival and military security of the Colony from a politically unstable neighbour (with the adjacent Province of Guangdong forming the volatile setting for much of the political struggle for national leadership in China).

A Hong Kong newspaper editorial defined the official attitude in Hong Kong and London throughout the period in question as being characterized by three strands of thought: a vague belief in the superiority of the past or of the status quo over the present; a dislike of interfering with local customs; and a general impatience with 'humanitarianism' and do-gooders in Britain as well as in Hong Kong.[8] On the other hand, there was no uniform Chinese attitude towards the mooi-jai custom. Moral sensibility was infinitely variable because subject to such factors as class, public status, and occupation.

It was the Chinese élite – members of which constituted the exclusive District Watchmen Committee, occupied seats in the Legislative Council, supplied the prestigious Tung Wah and Po Leung directorates – which exercised greatest influence on the Hong Kong Government's, and in turn on the Colonial Office's, perceptions and policies. In this view, the mooi-jai practice was born of philanthropic motives, in the absence of a tradition of social welfare provisions, whereby a young girl from a poor family was 'taken into' a wealthy household and in some instances, acquired kinship status equivalent to that of a daughter, if a somewhat inferior daughter. When reaching adulthood she would be given in marriage to a suitable partner, having served her master in gratitude for being saved from starvation or worse.

Deeply felt conservatism and traditionalism with regard to the position of women, and to the patriarchal structure as a whole, sought to stem the tide of new ideas about sexual relations, which saw the family as an agent of oppression of women. That the Chinese establishment in Hong Kong eventually gave its support to legislation abolishing the mooi-jai practice not only reflected on its impotence in the face of a resolute British Government, but also on the political complexion of Hong Kong's Chinese community.

In 1917, when the mooi-jai custom erupted as a public issue, spokesmen for the Chinese community were no longer confined to the élite. A growing professional class, including lawyers, doctors, accountants, and teachers, began to take part in the Colony's public life. It was this class of educated middle-class professionals that supplied the membership of the Anti-Mooi-Jai Society, established in 1921, a Society which saw itself in conscious opposition to the views propagated by the Chinese establishment.[9]

As for the representatives of the working population, the labour guilds, they were feared by the members of the Anti-Mooi-Jai Society as much as by the Chinese establishment and the British administration, and the guilds' pro-abolition stance came to play an important part in influencing decisions by the Chinese upper-classes and bourgeoisie to co-operate with the policy laid down by London. Chinese women, with few exceptions, played no part in the public debate.[10]

Those who conceived the Anti-Mooi-Jai Society did so because of their perception of the need to combat local reactionary forces which stood in the way of progress and social enlightenment. They demanded the liberation of mooi-jai as part of the general liberation of women, because, so the Society's publication stated, emancipation of all women was the *sine qua non* without which national welfare could not succeed.[11] The mooi-jai practice entailed bondage at its most oppressive, being slavery in essence.

While the perceptions of the typical élite Chinese were rooted in traditional assumptions about patriarchal prerogatives and evaluations of women, the perceptions of their opponents from the professional middle-class as to the nature of the mooi-jai custom had been influenced by developments which link up the history of its *de jure* abolition with a wider contemporary movement in Western countries towards the emancipation of women. The mooi-jai issue had come to acquire the dimensions of a cause, with all its symbolic overtones, which confronted the forces of progress (abolition) with political reaction, feudal oppression, and past-orientated thinking (the status quo).[12]

It is now necessary to turn from the realm of political perceptions, cultural reaction and new ideals to that part of the social canvas which contributed to the texture of the mooi-jai practice *per se*. The limitations of the legislative success eventually achieved by the pro-abolition campaigners (see Appendix A) can only be understood when it is realized that the phenomenon of the mooi-jai was intrinsically connected with a resistant patriarchal culture which was not open to change; that the mooi-jai practice fed on widespread, entrenched poverty among the labouring masses; that the victims carried with them the weight not only of physical oppression but also of psychological conditioning inducing a state of self-abnegation which would demand more than government decrees and proclamations to be rectified.

6. The Transaction[13]

To escape political and social disturbances, to escape poverty and starvation, men would seek work in the cities, or find protection and identity within secret societies – the women of the poor classes were more vulnerable in the face of vicissitudes.

Although urban areas had seen progress in the condition of women's lives (for example, in the abolition of foot-binding, in professional and educational opportunities) rural women were scarcely affected. Their vulnerability was due not only to a perpetuation of patriarchal values but also to the absence of economic opportunities, which maintained the time-honoured role with which women were still associated – to do with domesticity and reproduction, as well as sexual services. Thus patriarchal dicta, coupled with demands for unpaid domestic labour, for prostitutes and concubines, plus Chinese women's lack of general economic independence, contributed to a disparate situation: while educated Chinese women clamoured for political rights, women from the poorer social strata were still being sold into slavery.

Hong Kong was not only an entrepôt for inanimate goods between China and the rest of the world, but also for human beings. Girls of Chinese descent, born in Singapore, in the Dutch Indies, in the Straits, and in Macau were brought to Hong Kong for profit; girls from Shantou, Shanghai, Tianjin, and their rural hinterlands, were sold by way of Hong Kong to South-East Asian markets. All these girls shared a background of poverty, whether rural or urban. Some girls could recall farms on which the whole family had eked out a living; perhaps at some stage the family lost its tenancy, drifted to the nearest city, and during the phase of alienation from what had constituted the family's rootedness in social and moral values, the sale of the daughter might occur. Disassociation from a supportive context of kinship relations eroded many of the social inhibitions parents may have had in selling their daughters into an unknown fate.

In times of greatest desperation boys, too, were sold, mostly to be adopted; but this was always the last resort and an admission of ultimate defeat. Girls, being by cultural definition the 'outsider' in a patrilineal society, sooner or later to be married off to another family, went first. Patriarchal evaluation of the female sex, supported by the absolute authority of the *pater familias* to decide the fate of his family, provided for an obvious solution in times of material crisis: to sell the daughter, and grant the rest of the family at least a temporary respite.

At these times of crisis, parents, when parting from their daughters, were not always indifferent or callous to their fate. With the same reluctance, but resignation in the face of an unrelenting fate, with which families left their home-villages to face an unknown future in search of a living, they may have resorted to the next step in a downward spiral of despair, by offering their daughters on the market.

Age

The census report of 1921 recorded 8,653 mooi-jai in the Colony of Hong Kong.[14] Of this number 5,758 were under the age of 14 years and 2,535 were age 14 or over. Of them: 30% were under the age of 15, 25% under 17, 12% under 18, 8% under 19, and 5% were 19 and over. Few girls below the age of five were recorded as mooi-jai. Between the ages of 10 and 14 years the numbers were nearly equal for each age. The estimate was that above the age of 19 only about 150 girls were mooi-jai; the eldest recorded was 35 years of age.

A similar age distribution was revealed in a study of 65 cases of bei-nü, undertaken by the Shanghai Municipal Council in 1938.[15] Here too, the greatest density was to be found in the 11–15 and 16–20 age groups, with a slightly higher emphasis on the post 15 age group.

Table 6.1
Age distribution: 71 bei-nü

Age	Number
5	2
10–15	21
16–20	37
20–25	10
30 and over	1

Two points require discussion: firstly, although we may have a notion of age distribution at the time of the study, we are not given the ages of the bei-nü when they were bought; secondly, the impression might be received from the highest age group recorded for a mooi-jai that after she had reached a certain age she was no longer a mooi-jai; in other words, that *all* mooi-jai were liberated and their slavery terminated, when they came of age. I disagree with such a conclusion.

As for the first point, it is difficult to be quite certain, as no reliable data exist, and many mooi-jai I interviewed were unsure of their age at the time of transaction.

In Appendix B I have listed 61 cases of mooi-jai; from my study of court cases, in 35 cases the age at the time of transaction was given. The greatest density lies in the 10 to 14 age group, the next greatest in the five to nine age group.

Table 6.2
Age distribution: 35 mooi-jai

Age	Number
0– 4	7
5– 9	9
10–14	13
15–19	4
20 and over	2

The distribution of numbers in the age categories coincides approximately with the results of the investigations cited above. Because of the limited samples and problem of adequate representation for the total population of mooi-jai, generalizations must be highly tentative.

It appears that the purchase of a child under the age of five years was uncommon, and the purchase of a girl under the age of nine less common than of a girl aged between ten and 14 years. From the point of view of a purchaser this age would make economic sense. The mooi-jai could be considered old enough to do housework and look after children, but young enough to learn and to adjust to the master's family and a strange way of life. She could be exploited in her owners' household for a number of years, and if considered expedient, could be resold for other purposes before having passed the stage of youth so vital to purchasers of concubines and prostitutes.

Just one comment on the comparatively high percentage of infants (20%) being sold, as suggested by the table above, the youngest a mere five days old: as these transactions often occurred in Hong Kong, with the seller a resident of the Colony, they must be accounted for by the unspeakable poverty of the Hong Kong proletariat. The infant mortality rate, especially during the late 1920s and early 1930s, was constantly hovering around the 50% mark. Even taking into account the unreliability of the birth registration figures of that time, the very high percentage of deaths among Chinese infants reveals a particularly grim consequence of the poverty in pre-War Hong Kong.

As for the second point – did all mooi-jai gain their freedom at a certain age (the oldest mooi-jai recorded was 35 years)? – a number of interpretations can be given for which such statistical data cannot account. In 1921, when for the first time mooi-jai were recorded separately in a population census in Hong Kong, upper-class Chinese families were already aware of the beginnings of a campaign to abolish the mooi-jai institution and of its potential threat to their 'face'. It would therefore have been easy to list mooi-jai simply as domestic staff, or to send them to the mainland until the census-taking was over.

In middle- and lower-middle class families a mooi jai was often resold at an age when, in theory, she should have been married off. The statistics then would not include her, whether she had become a prostitute, a concubine, or a first wife. The assumption that it must have been the last factor that caused the termination of the mooi-jai status is, as I will try to show in the following sections, highly debatable. Upper-class families, which tended to keep mooi-jai in life-long service, therefore had at their disposal means for evading detection. With regard to lower-class families, which tended to resell their mooi-jai, being more dependent on the financial gain from such sale, the mooi-jai disappeared from view at an age when she was supposed to be set free from bondage. Statistical records did not enquire into the precise whereabouts of these mooi-jai.

The Go-betweens

'As without clouds in the sky it cannot rain, so without go-betweens a match cannot be made.'
(Chinese proverb)

In Chinese custom, the presence of a go-between and the contractual obligations recorded in a deed of sale, lent a binding quality to transactions. Chinese officials recognized the bargain as binding even, '... it appeared, where the child had been previously stolen, provided the purchaser had complied with the custom in getting a deed with the go-between as witness and agent. They would restore a runaway purchased servant to the vendee... '[16]

Go-betweens in general came from the class of pedlars, midwives, amahs, fortune-tellers, restaurant and teahouse staff; in other words, from that class with the greatest mobility in travelling between countryside and town, and mixing with classes likely to buy and sell children.

With regard to their social status the Hong Kong authorities declared:

Their social status is low, and the funds at their disposal at any one time are probably small. In fact, it is not unlikely that these persons are usually agents working on commission. Their employers may be individuals or possibly syndicates working through a Chinese boarding-house. In one case the method is believed to have been to advance money to these agents in return for a promissory note. No doubt credit is given by the boarding-house on the same terms.[17]

Go-betweens were usually women. Their life-styles and economic independence from men represented an anomaly in Chinese society and for that reason they have traditionally been looked upon with suspicion and mistrust. The typical go-between possessed a great deal of social knowledge gathered at her location of work, supplemented by her wide network of acquaintances (often travelling traders, hawkers, amahs) who brought her the latest gossip. She was used for many intimate transactions (for example, a wealthy man requiring the services of a young concubine, or prostitute) and acted as a confidante to many persons superior in class. Her position of access to 'inner-chambers' – the spheres inhabited by wives and concubines – permitted the invaluable collection of useful information and gave her power beyond her social station. Necessary, she was also feared; indispensable, she aroused resentment; well-known, she was never popular. Her characteristics were described to me as consisting of deviousness, shrewdness, independence, cunning, strength, and loud and vulgar behaviour. She was regarded as the very antithesis of respectable Chinese womanhood and, moreover, seen by men as a subversive influence which could corrupt unsuspecting innocent females.[18]

Her part in the transaction could consist of different levels of involvement. She could go to villages herself and buy young girls of a suitable age whom she then would take to her home in the city. The initial expenditure might come from her own capital or, as the above quotation suggests, might constitute an advance from the commissioning agent. Once returned home with her purchase she would announce the new arrival to potential buyers. In many instances she would dispose quickly of the 'goods', thus realizing an instant profit. But in this case the share would never be as large as when the girl had been trained by the go-between to attract buyers of concubines or high-class prostitutes. This meant keeping the girl or girls for a longer period of time and was possible only if the go-between had sufficient capital to tide her over the period of 'gestation'. I was told that these houses were generally called 'stables' and former members of such establishments came 'from the same walk'.[19] When working as a member of an organized gang the go-between's role was confined to receiving the object of transfer and establishing contact with potential buyers.

Many women did this work on a part-time basis, or as a one-time favour for their employer. Relatives might have told them of impoverished families in their home village and they would suggest a girl to their employer.[20] The better her contacts the more profit she could realize.

The important point is that the girl so kept could be transformed into a concubine, a prostitute, or a mooi-jai: for the go-between the decisive factor was the price offered. One could say that the go-between provided the bridge in the most essential contradiction between the 'haves' and the 'have-nots', those who had only themselves to sell.

On Prices

The price-level depended on so many variables including famines and the political and military situation in a specific region of China, which if bad could drastically reduce the price of children. In 'normal' times other factors, such as the severity of law enforcement regarding trafficking in children (and there were considerable regional variations),[21] the demand for fresh recruits for brothels, the beauty of an individual girl and the length of her training – all these factors would influence the fixing of the price. Calculations also related to age. Between Hong Kong $10 and $15 was paid for every year of a girl's age, that is, for a girl of four years old, $40 or $60 and so on.[22] In Africa, slave prices of females – because of their reproductive functions – were consistently higher than for males,[23] but generally this was not the case in China, where ancestor worship imposed its own priorities. The demand was for boys who could be adopted to continue the patriline.

In 1929, in connection with the discovery of an organized system of brokerage in children in Hong Kong, the press reported that:

These cases also disclosed that prices may range between $70 or $80 for a baby child and $500 for children of more mature age. Generally speaking, a boy commands the better price, as he is much fancied by those who are childless. And then his lot is a happier one than that of a girl, over whom many evils associated with the nefarious traffic hang heavily.[24]

Another way of looking at the question of price is to translate the price for a girl of a certain age, in a given year, into food and housing for the poor. There are some statistics available for the 1930s (see Table 6.3) on estimated *per capita* weekly food and fuel costs for Hong Kong and on the actual average income of the poor in Hong Kong; these figures were published twice a year by the Hong Kong Society for the Protection of Children.[25] I extracted the figures from press reports for 1931, 1932, 1934 and 1935. These I want to juxtapose with the average prices paid for children in order to get a contemporary perspective on the relativity of human value.

These are approximate estimates, based on equally approximate statistics for a selected number of years. But they give a sense of reality to the material options open, for example, to a parent in 1932 in Hong Kong, living off a subsistence income of $2.87 per month *per capita*. The price paid for a mooi-jai could average $100, which could keep a family of three going for a period of nearly 12 months!

In Appendix B I have listed 61 cases of transferred girls where age, destination, and price were all, or partially, known. At first glance the seemingly wide price fluctuations throughout the 1920s and 1930s do not appear to make for the recognizable patterns stated above. Although there is a slight increase in price as time goes on, in the late 1930s the prices suffer a definite slump. Also, within a specific year, prices for mooi-jai or prostitutes vary considerably; this is because prices were dependent on many outside factors. Prices in the late 1910s, late 1920s and late 1930s

Table 6.3

	January – June		July – December		
Year	Average monthly cost	Average estimated income	Average monthly cost	Average estimated income	Average child prices
1931	5.78*	3.8	5.892	Below 4	Moo-jai: 130 3-year-old moo-jai: 39
1932	5.628	2.87	na	na	Mooi-jai: 100 Sale into prostitution: 130
1934	4.1	2.47	na	na	Pledge for loan: 160 Pledge for loan: 100
1935	na	na	3.78	2.01	Boy (adopted): 35 Pledge for loan: 100

*Figures in Hong Kong $

indicate the presence of famines, of social and political instability and demographic upheavals which always increased the supply of children and made them available at times for mere pittances. In more normal times the designation of a girl for either domestic slavery, prostitution, or concubinage accounted for the price differentials, with prostitution and concubinage fetching higher prices. Yet there are differences in price within a certain time-span for the mooi-jai category, which are not explained by the age factor. This is because a girl sold as a mooi-jai might sometimes fetch a higher price because she might be suitable for lucrative resale. Between the first and second sale of certain girls the price shoots up remarkably. In 1929, for example, a 4-year-old girl was sold and resold within a short period of time; at the first sale she fetched $30, at the second $70. In 1929 a mooi-jai was bought for $100, a few months later she was sold for $140 (one has also to consider that these girls in the intervening period served their owners as domestic servants, and so on, so that the gain over and above this profit should be greater than the $40 given). It is this multiple use-value for the owners of transferred girls which created these discrepancies. These variants concealed the reality of a highly uncertain future for a girl thus transferred and starkly stated the boundaries of the cultural evaluation of Chinese women.

Deeds of Sale

As in other forms of transactions, transactions in children were recorded in detail in a document of sale, sung-tip, stating the intention of the parties to the transaction, the sum of money paid to the child's guardians, the unconditional or conditional nature of the right of ownership delegated to the buyer over the child, and the name of the go-between, and bearing the signatures or fingerprints of all parties involved in the sale. This was customary procedure in order to preempt suspicions of kidnapping and also to open the way for eventual resale (unless otherwise stated in the sung-tip) when documents were shown as evidence to claims of ownership over a given child.

But sung-tip were not always drawn up. From my interviews with upper-class Chinese, former employers of mooi-jai, I was given to understand that taking-in a poor girl was seen as an act of charity, a philanthropic gesture, in the context of which a sung-tip would have seemed 'out of place'. I was told that such a document would have denoted a binding obligation on the employer which, between members of classes of such different social standing, was inappropriate. An act of benevolence was permissible, but not a transaction suggestive of mutual reciprocity. *Geung-cho-ngan* (lit., ginger and vinegar money) was given as 'good luck money' which, ignoring the use-value of the girl for the family, made it seem an exercise in pure altruism.[26]

Documents were not drawn up in cases of clandestine sales or when sales took place in famine conditions, when the parents would sell the daughter to a trader without insisting on customary conventions. When in 1929 an amendment of the 1923 Female Domestic Ordinance enforced compulsory registration of mooi-jai, subsequent prosecution pertaining to the keeping of unregistered mooi-jai, and of 'adopted daughters', made these documents an important part of the habeas corpus of a case.

The colour of the paper used for a sung-tip depended on the nature of a transaction. When a daughter was adopted, red paper was common; white paper signified the transaction of a mooi-jai.[27] Red paper might also be used when the parties were good friends while white paper was common when a go-between was employed.[28] When, however, the mooi-jai practice became increasingly an object of legal prosecution and social opprobrium, the colour of the paper was often changed to red and the term 'mooi-jai' gave way to 'adopted daughter'! Thus these documents lost much of their fact-finding value; in instances when a transfer of the mooi-jai had been recorded on white paper but the master maintained it had been a case of adoption, the document became mysteriously lost or 'mislaid' never to be discovered again. Sung-tip also frequently turned out to be forgeries, in which sellers claimed to be the rightful guardians of children. Yet despite all these qualifications, the deeds of sale offer an interesting enough insight into the custom to make their study worthwhile.

In almost all cases the parents or guardians of a child (mostly coming from the poor and illiterate classes) had to employ either a literate go-between or a street-writer for the task of documentation, with the parties to the sale giving their fingerprints. In order to make the transaction truly watertight the document might be stamped at a police station. As late as 1929 a document of sale was found in Hong Kong, stamped by a Cantonese police officer.[29]

In the cities, documents were usually kept by the buyers; but when the sale took place in rural areas where the authority of the lineage was still intact, the document might be kept at the lineage hall.

Chinese informants generally made a distinction between a 'note of presentation' and a 'deed of sale'. The former often stated that the transfer of parental power was due to economic hardship; the payment of geung-cho-ngan was deemed a reimbursement for some of the expenditure on the girl. The new guardian's power was strictly circumscribed:

> After the child has been handed over to the Chung family, Chung Ying Liu will take good care of her, and when she comes of age, she will be married by order of Chung Ying Liu and at the same time her parents will be informed of her marriage so that they may have the right of visit thereafter.

In the case of a deed of sale, the wording is explicitly a sale-and-purchase terminology and the price paid, a purchase price, *san-ga-ngan*. The guardians fully renounce all their rights over and claims upon the girl, specifying the purpose of sale or leaving it within the competence of the new owner:

> After this sale, Chan Yee Koo [the buyer] shall have the right to change the name of the girl. If the girl is disobedient Chan Yee Koo shall be allowed to resell her, and the mother shall have no recourse. In the event of any misfortune befalling the girl, there is no blame to either party.

The natural parents state that no prior claim exists on the girl, and that, should difficulties arise, the buyer is in no way held accountable for them. 'It is also made perfectly clear that the girl has never been betrothed to any other family, nor is there any mortgage on her.' The note of presentation and deeds of sale (quoted in full in the Appendices C, D, E and F) feature all the basic elements constituting contracts of sale.

The Purchasers

There were three reasons for requiring girls. First, there was the concubine system which existed formerly in China; secondly, sale to prostitute houses; thirdly, and comparatively more fortunate for the girls, sale as *mui tsai*, or girl slave. Sometimes the girl sold as a concubine might be happy because married to a respectable, rich and good man. Girls of no education from the country might be disposed of their own free will to enter houses of prostitution. Girl slaves or mui tsai might be satisfied finding themselves more comfortable in the homes of their purchasers because they get better treatment there than in the homes of their parents.[30]

Because my case studies in this chapter are largely based on Hong Kong court cases and on cases that came to light in Guangzhou and Macau, it may seem that mooi-jai and others were recruited from the countryside exclusively for the urban areas of China and South-East Asia. This was not so. Many comfortably-off and well-to-do families in the villages of South China kept mooi-jai and concubines bought from the native village or neighbouring places. But the attraction of cities for country girls, the city anonymity enjoyed by traders in girls, the concentration of money and therefore higher prices paid for girls, made this city trend an important part of the 20th century trafficking in females. It was also in the cities that 'modern' abuses of overwork occurred and the bao-fan system, directly related to the system of transfer of children and women, emerged.[31]

The differing 'types' of purchasers I want to discuss in turn reveal much about the different treatment such transferred girls could experience, as well as the different expectations on the part of employers, which cannot be separated from their social station, material circumstances and cultural values.

Upper-class employers: Masters from this class were often local landlords or rich creditors to whom parents were obligated. Parents who could not afford to care for their daughters might also come and beg a rich family to take in their daughter, and in these families often two, three, or more mooi-jai might be kept. When a young mooi-jai was pretty, and attractive enough to appeal to the master or his son, she might, in due course, be taken as a concubine or she might be taken without being granted the official status of a concubine (this, by custom, involved the consent of the first wife, expressed in a ritual act of welcome). It was this class of employers that most often stressed the charitable nature of the mooi-jai institution, and the honour involved for those mooi-jai who were promoted to the status of a concubine.[32] The institution was seen as the embodiment of age-old philanthropy, which had saved poor girls from starvation 'and worse'. At this point a popular juxtaposition was introduced between upper-class benevolence and servants' dependable loyalty in the 'old days', and the contemporary situation of harassed employers compelled to pay exorbitant wages to 'unwilling and greedy servants'. From this perspective their perceptions were coloured by a nostalgia for past privileges of which keeping a mooi-jai had formed an integral part.

In these households the customary drawing up of a sung-tip, when a girl was taken in, tended to be disregarded. This same disregard applied to the, theoretically speaking, temporary nature of the mooi-jai status. My questions about the customary rights of the mooi-jai were greeted with astonishment, smiles, or derision.[33]

Once the girl had been taken in, she would be instructed in the tasks expected of her. In these homes paid servants did the menial and heavy work; the mooi-jai would either be delegated to care for the master's daughter, or his wife.[34] She might also be entrusted with some light housework. The link with her natal family rarely survived the first days as a mooi-jai. It was explained to me that as these girls grew accustomed to their new families they forgot about home. 'When the new family is better off and she now has a comfortable life and nice clothes, naturally she prefers to stay.'[35] According to those interviewed, the mooi-jai had 'lots of time, and often nothing to do at all'. They were treated 'as members of the family', had lots of space where they lived in the servants' quarters, and could play to their hearts' content; they spent much time 'just fooling around' with the master's children.[36]

It took long questioning before more concrete details about the mooi-jai's life were revealed. Although the mooi-jai did little heavy work, she was constantly at the master's beck and call. This meant fanning the mistress when she felt hot, filling the water-pipe, pouring tea, or just being present. Regardless of whether it was early in the morning or late at night, the girl's services were expected at a moment's notice. In most upper-class households the first wife and concubines tended to spend much time entertaining women friends to long sessions of mah-jong, sometimes lasting well into the early hours of the morning. As we have already noted, when the mooi-jai collapsed out of sheer exhaustion she might be beaten on the knuckles with chopsticks and made to stand up again.[37] Not only the mistress but the children too could provoke the mooi-jai to the point of tears, by subjecting her to cruel games or teasing.[38]

Once the mooi-jai had grown up and happened to be of pleasant appearance she frequently became the object of sexual attention. Mooi-jai were not uncommonly seduced by the master or his son;[39] if they were fortunate they might be promoted to become concubines. In some instances it happened that the wife or (first) concubine would fear a new rival and try to be rid of her before she grew too powerful. If she had been 'spoilt' already, she might be sold into a Hong Kong or Guangzhou brothel, earning for the mistress a large sum of money.[40] When the girl remained a mooi-jai, in exchange for 'saving a poor creature', such families would commonly expect life-long service. The girl's life would thus be indefinitely appropriated for the use of the master's family. Sometimes an affectionate and mutually devoted relationship would spring up, especially between mistress and mooi-jai; I was repeatedly told of 'love relationships' which survived the relationship between husband and wife.[41]

Not only did the mistress, in the course of a long relationship with her mooi-jai, become psychologically dependent on her for comfort, affection, and company, but her bound feet made her physically dependent on the support of her large-footed mooi-jai. A venerable member of the proud Ho lineage, a lively 91-year-old woman, displayed her bound feet with great pride; they were (and still are) an eloquent statement on her social status. She proclaimed to me that, 'a proper wife came from a good family and she always had bound feet'. Each of her nine sisters had bound feet and, when they were at an age when the bandages were bound tightly around their tender bones (she, herself, had been six years old then) each of them received a mooi-jai to look after personal needs. A friend of hers, the daughter of a wealthy comprador, had been presented with four mooi-jai to care for her needs: to be with her during wakeful nights of pain, and to carry her into the garden when her feet were too painful to walk on.

In these rich households the mooi-jai's position was ambiguous, depending on her standing in the master's family: she might be bullied by the servants or treated with cautious deference.[42] Mooi-jai whom I interviewed and who had stayed on with 'their' families had become mouthpieces of their masters: their views on life and of their own station in it a carbon-copy of their masters'. Their affection and dedication centred on the person whom they had served personally, sometimes for decades; but their identification extended to the whole family and their affairs, even to the lives of those members who had many years since left the family to work abroad or to marry and live in another part of the Colony. Mostly, the interviews were taken up by discussing the fate of each individual member of the household – their marriages, career prospects, number of children; when I tried to turn the conversation round to their own lives, I was greeted with a smile. They had already told me.

Yet, even where the treatment had been kind and humane, they still remained the property of their masters, in whose power it was to do with them as they pleased. Whether the treatment was kind or cruel, the true nature of the relationship as one of owner and owned was not affected.

Middle- and lower-classes: The cases which came before the Hong Kong law courts largely involved mooi-jai owners from the middle- and lower-classes. This was usually because upper-class Chinese either dealt with the potential social embarrassment by quickly disposing of the mooi-jai (by sale, or marriage), by sending them back to the master's ancestral home on the mainland, or by changing their status to one of a paid servant, an amah. The upper-class was less likely to be involved with the law, which for its effectiveness often depended on public scrutiny, anonymous information, or curious neighbours. Members of the upper-class would be most reluctant to upset the social equilibrium by causing another member of their class to 'lose face'; non-interference was a more characteristic mode of behaviour. Not one case reported in the Hong Kong press involved the élite.

The middle- and lower-classes made a precarious living in pre-War Hong Kong. Apart from a few Chinese men, employed on a fixed income by

Government departments, the majority of families were directly affected by the fluctuating state of Hong Kong's commerce and local industry – which suffered as much as the rest of the world from economic recession, protectionist policies and currency manipulation – but had to contend with the additional strain of regional political instability.[43] The fact that neither official welfare provisions nor extensive private, charitable institutions existed at the time, and that the first *kaifong*, providing for charity and immediate relief, was established only in 1949, in some measure helps one realize the economic strain under which these families lived.[44] The conditions of the mooi-jai's life with such families were, by implication, harsher than she would have experienced had she been purchased by a rich family.

She tended to be viewed as a business proposition. Her buyer would examine and discuss her as one discussed the merits of a work-horse; her teeth were inspected, and she underwent a medical examination to assess her potential work-performance in the household.[45] Very rarely was there the division of labour which existed in upper-class households, where mooi-jai might be responsible for only a specifically allocated part of the general domestic work. In middle- and lower-class households the mooi-jai was responsible for child-care and housework, often involving heavy physical strain. Certainly there were graduations; in a successful merchant's household several mooi-jai might be employed and the greater leisure of the women called for more personal services. The more precarious the financial standing of the family, the fewer the servants, the more wide-ranging the tasks taken on by the mooi-jai, the more separate her life became from the master's family and the harsher the treatment she received from mistress and master.

Many court case reports did not specify the occupation of the employer, referring either to a 'well-dressed middle-class woman', to a 'well-to-do man', or simply to a ' married woman'. In this class the resale of mooi-jai for greater profit was common (at times of financial crisis or hardship, for example). The concubine in an upper-class family might secretly dabble in the business of selling mooi-jai, but in the middle- and lower-middle classes such trading went on much more openly. With less ideological cloaking of the custom, the mooi-jai was seen as a cheap way of getting household help and also as an asset to be realized if necessary. Typical of this attitude was the case before a Hong Kong court in 1921, when a middle-class woman was charged with persistent cruelty towards her 13-year-old mooi-jai. The girl had suffered from stomach trouble, and when in this condition was unable to wash the family's linen. Then she would be kicked and beaten by the mistress and accused of stealing family property (such accusations of theft were very frequent). The mistress addressed the girl in the court:

'You were sick when I bought you. I had to go to such expense in engaging the five doctors that had been called to see to your condition, and now you would be so ungrateful as to go to the Police and give evidence against me.' When the magistrate asked what right she had to beat the girl, the woman said 'I did not beat her much.' 'You did not beat her much, look at her face,' the magistrate retorted. The defendant: 'She was sick'.[46]

This mooi-jai could not live up to the expectations of her mistress, therefore she became redundant and an object of contempt. This was not an isolated case. When questioned about the treatment of mooi-jai and if it was comparable to the treatment of a daughter, the wife of a merchant and former employer of mooi-jai replied, 'You think they were invited to a picnic?'[47] Not that these families lacked compassion for the mooi-jai's lot, but lack of financial security narrowed the options for charitable impulses. In all my interviews, the nature of Hong Kong society and its effect on social relations was emphasized as having been 'bad' and very different from what was important in relationships on the mainland, as if in coming to live and work in Hong Kong the last vestiges of altruistic behaviour were erased to fit in with an environment conducive to behaviour that was competitive, self-interested, profit-motivated, and callous toward others' needs. Whether this was the perception of life in Hong Kong as they had found it, or whether it served as a rationalizing device for a way of life devoted to materialistic goals is debatable. Perhaps the pressure of Hong Kong life left little leeway to do otherwise. Either way, in this mental and physical environment the mooi-jai institution carried only the faintest similarity to the charity of old alleged to constitute its *raison d'être*.

Advocates of the 'charitable' mooi-jai institution also insisted that because it served to relieve the poor from the burden of supporting useless daughters, no poor family kept mooi-jai. Had it been such a charitable institution this would have been correct; but press reports of court-cases tell of the unemployed or coolies with mooi-jai who had to sleep outside the family cubicle in corridors because there was no space inside. Childless couples would buy girls for purposes of *fuk si*, that is, service. Not wealthy enough to purchase a son, they purchased a girl, hoping thus to secure later a son-in-law who would be willing to look after them in old age and in bad times.[48] It is difficult to give a numerical estimate of cases of relatively poor buyers of mooi-jai. From the evidence I have read I would, however, speculate that in times when a mooi-jai was cheap and might be had for little or nothing, such acquisition might be considered a useful asset for later contingencies. It is in this light that the practice of keeping mooi-jai must be seen. When such cases came before the court, often with charges of maltreatment, the mistress would maintain that the girl refused to eat, and only belatedly acknowledge that the family was poor and could not afford more than two meals per day of which the mooi-jai would get little.[49]

Cruelty often came from the mistress, who, under the strain of working to keep the family (possibly supplementing the family income as a hawker, or helping in street stalls) and looking after the family, surviving frequent pregnancies, would be most likely to vent her anger and tension on the mooi-jai.

An additional source of victimization for the mooi-jai was what the Anti-Mooi-Jai Society called the 'nasty habits and superstitious outlook prevailing in the Chinese family'.

Even the trivial thing like sweeping the floor or making a pot of tea has some superstition attached. It is unlucky, for instance, for the mui tsai to sweep from the back of the house outward towards the front door. The proper way is to sweep a few times at the door first before collecting all the dirt into the dustbin. The other method of sweeping, according to the dictates of superstition, amounts to driving all the precious wealth and good fortune from the family and household.

Should the mui tsai fail to observe this mere trifle, and accidentally point the broom at any member of the family, it would invite misfortune. In making tea it is a bad omen to point at anybody with the bottom of the hot water boiler [kettle?]. Imagine a mui tsai of 9 or 11 years of age is expected to bear in mind these trivial beliefs, or there will be more birching for her.[50]

7. Mooi-jai

> Girls are everywhere openly bought and sold for maidservants or slaves, the euphemism *yang nü* "adopted girl", usurping the place of *pei nü* so offensive to the ear of the law, and their use as domestic slaves in the families of well-to-do Chinese is too common to call for comment, except on the rare occasion when inhuman treatment occasioning the death or injury of some unfortunate girl is brought to light.[51]

What was the mooi-jai's realm of duties and obligations, what was her relationship with the master's family and her natal family, and what ritual obligations arose from this relationship?

Lucy Ching, a young Chinese girl growing up in pre-War Guangzhou, once inquired of her amah the difference between her status and that of a mooi-jai. The amah explained she had freedom of movement, choice of leaving or staying in a current employment, negotiation of pay – she continued:

> A female slave could not do anything like this. Once she was sold by her family she would have to work for the same master or mistress all her life, without pay, unless her owner chose to sell her or give her away. As she grew older the decision as to whether she should be married, and to whom, would rest entirely with her owner.[52]

The question was often asked in the discussion about the status of a mooi-jai: was she like an adopted daughter? A cynical interpretation of the possible connection between the two was given to me by a direct descendant of a mooi-jai:

> The term of 'adopted daughter' is usually used when the mooi-jai has got rich or powerful (usually as a concubine) and that was the case of my grandma; the mooi-jai of mother's stepsister... they would class the mooi-jai as adopted daughters when they were sold off as concubines to rich Chinese in Malaya.[53]

Thus, when a mooi-jai had acquired wealth and influence through a powerful husband, a former master or mistress might change her status to the more intimate term of *yeung nui*, suggestive of a continuous and permanent relationship between foster-parent and daughter.

In cases when the mooi-jai found herself upon marriage in humbler circumstances, she might be quickly forgotten. This happened to Sun-mui, the mooi-jai of Chan Kam-yang, who was married to a tailor. Sun-mui avoids all contact now because the former mistress 'only associates with rich and wouldn't have time for people like her.'[54]

Work

If a mooi-jai was acquired by an upper-class family her work differed from that required of her in middle- or lower-class families. I have already elaborated on the former (see Chapter 6) and here I shall discuss the majority of mooi-jai who worked for the middle and lower income groups.

In these households domestic work and care of children were the most important tasks. Sometimes the work was heavy, such as carrying water, or barrels of pigfood, or doing the family's washing. The mooi-jai worked long hours, and rarely had opportunity for recreation or education – so that these girls grew up in ignorance of the world, tying them ever more deeply to the master. Time spent shopping was closely supervised and scarcely permitted more than a brief exchange of words with the traders at the market, or with an acquaintance passing by in the street.

Mooi-jai were under a heavy strain – not only did they have to work hard, but they were subject to a constant barrage of criticism by often tense and short-tempered mistresses. Court-cases tell of chastisement meted out upon slightest provocation. Upsetting a bucket of water could bring severe beatings. Spilling rice caused major flare-ups of temper. The poorer the household the more instances of cruelty were brought to light at the law courts.

In 1932, the owner of a mooi-jai, a Public Works Department coolie, was fined $75. The girl had to get up at 3 am to cut grass, do the housework, clean out the pig-sties, and so on. She had very little sleep, received no wages, took her meals alone and had to eat what was left over from the family's meal. When she fell ill, she could not do the expected amount of work and was punished with beatings and kickings. When the case was discovered – the girl stood crying in the street – she had to be put into hospital, suffering from a breakdown. Upon investigation it was found that her parents had also sold her two brothers and two sisters, allegedly being unable to sustain the family.[55]

Women rather than men seemed to excel in cruelty to their mooi-jai. Favourite punishments were beating with the handle of a feather duster or a split cane, burning with heated tongs or lit matches, tying up the mooi-jai for long hours, not giving her food. Catalogues of cruelty could be given about women whose only available outlet for pent-up emotions was the mooi-jai. A considerable number of concubines in the middle-class stratum of Chinese society stood before the magistrates accused of maltreating their slave-girls. The explanation given to me was that concubines were raised by amahs, had little education (meaning 'moral' education) and therefore were more likely to abuse their power over their vulnerable 'toy'.[56]

In view of the unlimited power over the mooi-jai it is not surprising to read of the various ways they could be made use of. They were loaned out to friends, with the earnings kept by the master; they were sent to markets to sell produce, again with the income kept by the master; they were sent begging or could be shared out among relatives to save employing paid labour.

Lax factory codes in Hong Kong, and their absence in South China, permitted the employment of girls of 12 years and upwards to work nightshifts. This, too, lent itself to abuse, and a stricter and more rigidly applied factory code was demanded in order to stem the spread of this form of labour.[57] In 1936, Agatha Harrison (Women's International League) stated before the Mui Tsai Commission in Hong Kong that in a survey of working conditions of women and children in China and Hong Kong she had discovered mooi-jai who had been sent to the factories by their owners.[58]

Wages

Mooi-jai started to receive wages only when registration began in December 1929. Up to the age of 14 years they were to receive $1 per month; from the age of 15 years onwards they were to receive $1.50.[59] Agnes Smedley remarked (in 1930) that the fact that the British Government of Hong Kong had fixed wages on behalf of mooi-jai was a tacit recognition that mooi-jai were not free to determine their wages, unlike, for example, amahs.

It was difficult to enforce the payment of wages. Unless the mooi-jai herself informed the visiting inspector, the master's word had to be accepted. Even registered mooi-jai might receive no money because the mistress would ask her to pay off the purchase-price received by her parents.[60] Sometimes the mistress would defend non-payment of wages by maintaining that the girl demanded nothing more than food and clothing. In other instances a girl, presented by a debtor to a creditor for repayment of a loan, would not be registered as a mooi-jai. Instead she was presented as an 'adopted daughter'.

Even those girls whose masters had registered them and who were under SCA supervision were still subject to numerous manipulations. As long as the mooi-jai remained within the relationship of 'buyer and bought' (and the interposition of $1 made little difference) the psychological and social pressures on her showed up the farcical nature of the so-called 'liberation' of the mooi-jai.

Marriage gifts were sometimes given to the mooi-jai from the money paid to her master by a suitor, but how frequently this happened is difficult to estimate. A former mooi-jai told me that she, and others she knew, never received anything. According to her it was more likely that the mooi-jai was the marriage gift presented to the daughter of the house.[61]

Mooi-jai's clothing was usually worn-out garments belonging to the mistress or her daughters. Most remembered that the clothes they had to wear were 'filthy and old': the express manifestation of their inferiority. When Miss Wei (an SCA inspector) walked along Hong Kong streets in the 1930s she would look out for girls 'with a certain shabby appearance', whose clothes and face indicated the treatment which made mooi-jai so unlike adopted daughters.

In the majority of cases the mooi-jai ate and slept with other servants (when there were any) and if they took their meals with the family it was often at a separate table, to be available when the family required their service.

Natal Family

Only in the interviews of mooi-jai by the Mui Tsai Commission of 1937 did I discover evidence that 'from time to time' one mooi-jai saw her parents; another mooi-jai said that her parents 'occasionally visited' her.[62] The other three girls interviewed at the time did not mention this point. The reason for the rarity of parental visits (unless the mooi-jai worked in the native village) was poverty, which prevented long journeys. Illiteracy prevented correspondence by letter and mooi-jai generally affected indifference to renewed contacts with their families – whose fate was often unknown to them. I suspect that the seeming indifference may have been more an acceptance of a given situation than a true indicator of family sentiment. In cases of enticement of a mooi-jai away from her owner, the means was often the promise to restore her to her parents. Girls who went to a police station to complain about the treatment they received usually expressed a wish to return home.

Upper-class Chinese and former owners of mooi-jai often told me that the 'Chinese are philosophical and pragmatic in their outlook' and when the mooi-jai found a better home and greater comfort with their master they were glad to be allowed to forget the discomforts of their previous life of poverty. It did not occur to such informants that very often the girls had no alternative but meekly to submit to a fate which must have seemed irreversible – without ever forgetting how they had started off in life.[63]

Registration

For many girls the stipulation under the 1929 amended Female Domestic Ordinance, that registration of mooi-jai was obligatory, had little effect on their lives. The number of missing registered mooi-jai was high, so must have been the number of unregistered mooi-jai. It is difficult to be exact about how many mooi-jai out of the actual total number in Hong Kong were discovered by the law.

On 31 May 1936, 1,723 mooi-jai remained on the register out of 4,368 who had been included on it before it was closed, in 1930. The following reasons were given for the 2,645 girls who had been struck off the register:[64]

died	46
returned to parents, etc	628
disappeared	244
left colony permanently	692
married	608
earning own living	312
taken into SCA custody	83
removed from register	26
other reasons	6

The whereabouts of 811 of 1,723 mooi-jai left on the register was unknown; many of them had never been visited. The number of mooi-jai then under inspection was 912.

Prosecutions of the owners of 164 girls, from 1 July 1930 to 31 May 1936 were for the following reasons:[65]

rape	1
conspiracy to procure a girl for carnal connection	1
gross cruelty	3
ill treatment or assault	25
failure to pay wages	23
failure to report changes	111

This last table does not include prosecution for employing unregistered mooi-jai or for bringing them into the Colony. During the same period 216 successful prosecutions for keeping unregistered mooi-jai and for bringing them into the Colony were recorded. The charges of ill treatment or assault were largely in respect of unregistered mooi-jai.

These statistics present considerable problems. They were given as part of the majority report (1937 MUI TSAI Commission) and were interpreted by the Commission to mean that the problem of mooi-jai in Hong Kong no longer existed. In commenting on the statistics the author of the minority report commented:

Its value depends upon an unknown quantity, i.e., the numbers of unregistered mui tsai. If there are only a few hundred, the number of prosecutions then is very satisfactory. If on the other hand there is a much larger number, the figures are not impressive.[66]

In August 1918 the Governor of Hong Kong reported to the Secretary of State that practically every Chinese household which could afford it had a mooi-jai. The Honourable Chow Shou-Son stated in the Legislative Council on 28 December 1922 that there were 'about 10,000 mui tsai in Hong Kong'. The 1921 population census reported 8,653 mooi-jai. At the same time that press reports recorded an increase in the traffic in children, not a single prosecution had taken place under the 1923 Ordinance. On 1 December 1929, the register opened for six months; by April 1930 less than 300 mooi-jai had registered. By the end of May, following dissemination of anti-mooi-jai propaganda, 4,252 mooi-jai were registered. The register closed on 1 June 1930, and the Governor of Hong Kong claimed success, referring to previous figures as exaggerated and 'a mere guess'. Did the 'mere guess' also refer to the population census of 1921, recording 8,653 mooi-jai, when already masters had begun to call their mooi-jai 'adopted daughters', because for three years British campaigners had taken up the issue with the assistance of the local press?

Moreover, the population during all this time increased rapidly; the female population alone increased by 125,584. Taking a normal percentage there should have been over 12,000 mooi-jai in Hong Kong in 1930. The gap between the official estimate of 'a few hundreds' and the 10,000 or 12,000 estimated by the minority report was therefore considerable.[67]

The mooi-jai I interviewed had never even heard of registration, although they had lived in Hong Kong as mooi-jai and afterwards as married women.[68] Kowloon and the New Territories of Hong Kong, where they had spent all their life, had been scarcely penetrated by the SCA inspectors. For the whole of the Colony only three inspectors carried responsibility and paid on average 2,978 visits per year.[69] Only after the war did the SCA employ ten women inspectors. One inspector, Miss Wei, admitted the huge problem of adequate coverage, that it had barely been possible to look after the registered mooi-jai; the detection of unregistered ones was a rare event. Generally, the Chinese public displayed an attitude of non-interference, in accordance with the popular motto, 'let each family look after its own affairs and take no notice of the frost on the neighbour's roof'.

According to Miss Wei, only about ten reports per year were made by the Chinese population. This, coupled with the ambivalent attitude of the Hong Kong administration towards the abolition of mooi-jai, made registration little more than a cosmetic exercise, something even the later Ordinance of 1938 would not resolve.

Termination

As to the question of when the mooi-jai ceases to be a mooi-jai, if at all, a 1935 Commission commented:

> A mui tsai is as free to leave her employer as any maid-servant employed by the hour. The mui tsai has no status and is under no contract enforceable by law. In the case of a mui tsai coming of age, 18 years, any person or institution could make an application to the Secretary of Chinese Affairs on behalf of a mui tsai.[70]

In practice the situation was by no means so simple. Especially in upper-class families with their code of loyalty and life-long devotion to the employer, the constant refrain was, 'our mooi-jai never married, they stayed with the family all their life'. What usually happened in these families was that if the mooi-jai did change her status, it was to become a concubine of the master. This meant that she posed little threat to the power position of the first wife and the other concubines, as her former status of mooi-jai would not be quickly forgotten. The past subservient position would have trained the girl to smoothly assume an inferior position among the women in the household; the outcome of a struggle for power was much harsher and more unpredictable when an outsider was taken in.[71]

Where a mooi-jai was redeemed, the owner could ensure he made a handsome profit, as the Anti-Mooi-Jai Society pointed out:

> As an example, if a slave girl is sold for $60, the owner can and will force the poor mother or seller to insert in the sale or 'presentation-card', as it is called in Chinese, the sum of $120 especially if the terms are on the basis of being able to redeem the girl in the future. There is certainly very little kindness shown in such Shylock-like method of exacting the pound of flesh.[72]

The choice of a marriage-partner for the mooi-jai was almost exclusively motivated by money considerations. Their prospective husbands might come from the class of tailors, shopkeepers, hawkers and the like, and often be considerably older than the girl. This is understandable as young men could scarcely afford the bride-price.

Often, if the marriage price offered was not high enough, masters would sell the girls into prostitution. In the cases examined by the League of Nations Commission of 1932, 13 out of 50 mooi-jai had been first adopted as daughters, then resold profitably, occasionally several times. In the other cases the relationships were not clear; many were sold by relatives and also made to prostitute themselves for the benefit of those relatives. Such actions were motivated by greed and the desire for commercial profit.[73]

A mooi-jai was constantly threatened with the prospect of being resold. I was told that such threats were used in cases of their 'bad deeds', or if they proved too troublesome and quarrelsome.[74] I was also told that out of 'goodwill' a master would sell his mooi-jai to a friendly family for less money than she might otherwise have brought. In court cases it was found that employers resold several of their mooi-jai into prostitution.[75] Once put into brothels or kept by women, who lived off their earnings, it was difficult for these girls to escape that life before their charms and youthfulness had been fully exploited.

Young girls, often infants, could not make use of British legislation in Hong Kong; usually because they knew nothing, or very little, about its existence. Even in the 1930s, when, under the impact of propaganda, public opinion began slowly to shift in favour of abolition, mooi-jai would rarely complain to the police. A maltreated child would live in fear, and this fear would prevent her from leaving – who would have protected her against the master's revenge? What were the alternatives? Parents, who had sold her once already, might sell her again; moreover, the parents' whereabouts might be unknown to the girl. The few charitable homes for girls without kin, like the Po Leung Kuk, were generally regarded with horror.

My interviewees repeatedly stressed the fear of authority: 'Even today (1978) Chinese do not go to the police, they treat you like dirt.' Even if people were only witnesses, they feared that in the time-honoured tradition of Chinese criminal law procedures, they might end up as the accused. How much more so, I was told, did this apply to young girls.

The decision as to what should be done with the mooi-jai, once she had reached adulthood, was invariably decided in terms of the master's, not the mooi-jai's, interest. The typical moralizing attitude was represented by a Chinese writer who exclaimed, 'did the government think about what will happen to the girls over 18 if they are allowed to be free by then to face this sinful world which is unknown to them?'[76]

Here, the writer, Wai Fung, was thinking not only of mooi-jai, but also of women in general, unfit to lead lives independent of their masters – whether in the capacity of owners of mooi-jai, guardians, fathers, or husbands.

'Typical' Personality of a Mooi-jai

Court-cases contained interesting comments by masters, mistresses, and their defence lawyers, about the characters of the girls in question. The following list of the girls' characteristics reads like an inversion of what were considered the attributes of respectable females excelling in the virtues of filial piety and obedience, reticence, loyalty, literal adherence to prescribed conventions. Mooi-jai were commonly described as stupid and ungrateful, they were thieves, they were licentious (playing with men in the streets instead of doing the shopping), they were wayward (slyly frequenting brothels) not coming home in time, were untrustworthy, troublesome, wilful, and always hungry and ate too much.

Considering the 'wilful behaviour' mooi-jai were accused of, the number who went to police stations to complain about their conditions, and who might have taken advantage of public sentiments, was negligible.

The Anti-Mooi-Jai Society's list of mooi-jai cases contains few examples of complaints brought by the mooi-jai. (It is not possible to estimate how small this proportion may have been, as most cases never came to light.) In 1921, one mooi-jai went to a police station to lodge a complaint about maltreatment. In 1923, two mooi-jai registered complaints; one after having received a brutal beating, the other in order to escape from prostitution. Five complaints were made in 1926 (all mooi-jai alleged maltreatment); few complaints by mooi-jai are known to have occurred in 1928, and few went to the police in 1929 – at a time when renewed agitation had brought the mooi-jai debate back into the headlines.[77]

The common denominator was despair: a mooi-jai could be driven to the end of her endurance by brutal beating, continuous maltreatment, the pressure to marry a wealthy but obnoxious man, by the threat that she might be sold into prostitution. What the master saw as a 'wilful' act, for her constituted a necessary, and all too rare, act of independence.

One must imagine how the young mooi-jai must have felt – anxious and frightened – when transferred to an alien environment, strange people, and an urban surrounding – unalleviated by parental affection and the security of home – for which their rural upbringing had left them unprepared. From the medical evidence presented at court cases we know that she was seen often as mentally deficient, and with 'a tendency to absent-mindedness'.[78] Many were described as callous and unable to relate to anyone and anything. It is interesting that these descriptions were often occasioned by a mistress's accusation that the mooi-jai had committed acts of theft in her house. One mistress had hidden herself in a clothes-basket, after placing a hand bell in a coat, and thus succeeded in catching the girl *in flagrante delicto*. At the Secretariat for Chinese Affairs, the girl expressed a desire to go home to her parents; in the court she stated she wanted to return to the master and mistress. When the magistrate pointed out the conflicting statement, the mooi-jai replied, 'anything will do'; she was sent to the Po Leung Kuk to 'better herself'.[79] It was 1921, but the magistrate did not think it necessary to address himself on the subject of 'callousness' to the mooi-jai's owner.

Death and Mourning

The observation of mourning rituals in Chinese society served to define and affirm boundaries of kinship ties through application of the *wu fu* (literally, the five kinds of mourning dress). More than mere expressions of differing degrees of blood relations, its principles of submission and devotion –

considered so important that the Codes of Law of all dynasties recognized the wu fu as legally binding – underlay the very organization of Chinese social structure.[80] Or, as Arthur Wolf maintained, the mourning dress did not so much 'reflect generalised kinship statuses, but is rather a reflection or declaration of rights in property.'[81] The severity of the mourning dress and an individual's length of mourning did thus mirror the nature of his (never her) access to ancestral property and ritual obligations. That blood-ties were, indeed, less decisive is evidenced by the fact that adopted sons mourned like natural sons.

> That the mourning rescripts were based in the first place upon the duty of being submissive to the chiefs of the family, and that the ideas about ties of blood played merely a secondary part in them, is rendered specially conspicuous by the precept that a child must mourn for its step-mother in just the same degree as for its own mother.[82]

In a patrilineal society the most strict mourning was prescribed for a dead patriarch by his eldest son or son of the eldest son. But the wu fu insisted upon a correct degree of mourning for all kin, whether they were of the older, younger, or of the same generation as oneself.

In the reality of Hong Kong the wu fu was observed in a more flexible fashion; this was particularly true of the poorer population – unable to give the time and afford the expenses such funerary rites required.[83] Most often neglected was the principle of mourning for a junior person. The mourning for an unmarried daughter depended to a large extent on the affection for her and the wealth of a family to give expression to their bereavement.[84]

The Chinese lawyer, Dr Ts'o, stated in a legal opinion that a mooi-jai 'mourned like a daughter'.[85] The British sociologist, Maurice Freedman, found that in Singapore the practice of mooi-jai was a form of adoption.[86] In my investigations I encountered only one former mooi-jai who told me in an interview that she had mourned for her deceased master as his own daughter had mourned. Other informants simply affirmed that mooi-jai in Hong Kong were under mourning obligations such as did not apply to hired servants.

Unlike in Singapore, in Hong Kong the mooi-jai was not an 'adopted daughter' but a useful slave. When the mooi-jai mourned she did not thus express her right to a dowry of the estate of the deceased, nor did she venture to give visible expression to affinal ties. As the Dutch sinologist De Groot saw it, the principles of submission and devotion that upheld the social organism of Chinese society required their constant renewal and validation in the rituals surrounding the death of a senior member of the family.

The mooi-jai was a possession which had been purchased and acquired for the use of her master. As the former mooi-jai told me, when she went through the motions of mourning which she had been instructed to observe, she felt she was subjected to the final gesture of ownership over her by the dead – and already to the first claim over her by the heir to the estate of the deceased. Her mourning was of the kind that slaves must have felt when in antiquity they were buried alive in their master's grave. Their 'mourning' served as outward symbol of status and proprietorship. They were the property.

When a mooi-jai died, even if she were owned by a wealthy family, it was more often than not a pauper's grave for her. In 1921, the 12-year-old Xiuling was a slave-girl owned by a family in a wealthy part of Hong Kong. She was brutally treated and badly burnt. On one particular occasion she was so sadistically beaten that she fainted and lay on the floor, seemingly dead. The mistress handed her over immediately to be buried in the hills. Because it was already dark, the caretaker left the coffin to be buried the next morning. But as he was digging the grave he heard sighing and crying and upon opening the coffin, the girl was discovered still alive. As the coffin had been too small for her, she had been simply pressed into it – adding yet more injuries. She was taken to a hospital which refused to hand the girl over to her owner.[87]

In 1922, a girl was buried in the 'dead box' after committing suicide – the box came from the Tung Wah Hospital. When asked by the police about the cause of suicide, the mistress maintained the girl had been an adopted daughter; the Anti-Mooi-Jai Society protested and claimed that other arrangements would have been made, 'if a burial consistent with the dignity of a daughter of a respectable household was desired.'[88] In two other cases related to me, the families – both wealthy – had left it up to the Tung Wah Hospital, a charitable institution for the poor, to make arrangements for burial. The families did not concern themselves further with the dead.

Conclusion

Less than 100 years ago, Moot Xiao-li was born into a poor and uprooted family to be sold at an early age. Little more than 40 years have passed since Ma Xin purchased a mooi-jai, when legally, both in China and in Hong Kong, the mooi-jai had ceased to exist. Shortly afterwards, in 1949, the People's Republic of China was founded which made the quest for equality between the sexes an integral part of the claim to engage in the construction of a socialist society. Since then new generations of women have grown up.

The commercial trade in women, the perennial concomitant of natural and man-made calamities before 1949, has in the main been eliminated. The commercial trader in women, the professional go-between in the transaction of women, the purchasers of women – they have largely gone, maybe for good. Instead of institutionalized domestic drudgery, prostitution, and contract labour, women have been granted a substantial and acknowledged part in economic production. Their rights as free and full citizens are guaranteed by the laws of the country. No one openly challenges the already proverbial saying that 'women can hold up half of the sky'. Indeed, so much is the idea of women's social equality anchored in the national consciousness of socialist China, that to question it is tantamount to questioning the whole edifice of China's belief system.

So few are the doubts about the nature of progress towards full equality that women's organizations and individual women rarely, if ever, confront the validity of public dogma in the private realm, where women face the source of a most entrenched traditional oppression. It is in this private sphere that economic and political changes must be complemented by a reform of the family structure and women's position in it, unless a terrible irony should be perpetuated – the irony that women's growing contribution to the public wealth of the country is not so much a consequence of their liberation from the fetters of old but a result of still greater additional burdens. What makes the necessary changes so difficult to realize is that success is dependent on progress in inner – that is, mental – processes where norms and values, conventions and traditional assumptions, define the place of women and their function in society. It is here that the bondages circumscribing women's lives are still more real and immediate to them than the rights granted as a consequence of their participation in the public sphere of society. It is here that the culture is most conservative and resistant to challenges. It is here that continuity with the lives of women in pre-1949 China – treating Hong Kong's Chinese society as its extension – is thrown into sharpest relief.

A woman's role, stipulated as domestic, is still interpreted for the convenience of society. Her territory is still mapped out in servicing labour, and most importantly, in producing the labour force (sons), heirs to the public duties and obligations transmitted by so many generations of ancestors. As in the older patriarchal society, on the woman's womb are still centred society's hopes and disappointments. Chance could give her sister in the society before 1949 a respected station in life, chance could deprive her of sons or make her barren – when she became as 'cheap as a doormat' – a target for ridicule and pity, vulnerable to maltreatment by her family or to sale into prostitution. Her modern sister is no longer faced with the more extreme vicissitudes of fate, but she, too, is judged by the parameters of fertile motherhood and loyal wifehood that applied to women of earlier ages.

The fatal assumption, preventing the emergence of a necessary critical consciousness in women, holds that socialism automatically connotes female emancipation. This assumption precludes a woman-focused examination of history which must be the first step towards an exploration of ideals of emancipation and equality, of the sources of real strength which women have displayed under the most adverse circumstances, and of the obstacles women have to overcome to prevent past patterns of oppression from repeating themselves.

The sale and barter of females – that is, the practice of mooi-jai – was one of the starker manifestations of a deeply entrenched gender inequality in Chinese culture which is still to be eradicated both in China and in Hong Kong. What women may need to realize is that there are still aspects of their lives which are but the threads in an ever-enduring social texture of patriarchal values which – unless radically severed – will continue to bind them to the practice of old when girls could be sold with impunity.

* * *

On a hot summer's day I looked up the family here in Guangzhou – as I had promised to do when I last saw Helen Chan. I am playing a go-between in a transaction which had its beginning in another century.

In the 1840s a small girl was sold by her father in Macau and brought to Guangzhou to be raised and trained by her new owner. She joined the company of four other mooi-jai, but at a riper age was sold as a concubine to a wealthy Hong Kong comprador. This girl was Helen's grandmother; the owner was the aunt of the head of the family whom I visited in Guangzhou. The transactions in girls had brought the aunt, Yip Min-yuk, sufficient wealth to enable her to invest in profitable Hong Kong shares. Later, the mother of my friend Helen had taken on the responsibility of managing the financial affairs on behalf of Yip Min-yuk's descendants (her brother's sons).

Long ago, Yip Min-yuk had granted her brother one of her mooi-jai to be his concubine. This former mooi-jai fell in love with her eldest step-son, and the incestuous pair frequently travelled to Hong Kong to stay at the house of that other former mooi-jai, Helen's grandmother, Moot Xiao-li. They were financed out of Yip Min-yuk's legacy. The couple accepted the ostentatious hospitality they received at Helen's grandmother's house as a mark of respect for the family of her former owner.

When the border closed between Hong Kong and China after 1949, the money-flow stopped. Since then Helen's mother, Chan Kam-yang, has been rewriting her own past and that of the nature of her mother's relationship with the family in Guangzhou. In these last 40 years the owner has become a 'foster-mother' to Moot Xiao-li, Helen's grandmother, and the contract turned into a one-way relationship of gifts and favours. Now, Helen's mother, on behalf of her family, received the *kow-tow* of both the legitimate branch of the Meng family and also the poorer relatives from her mother's side of the family.

She is dying slowly in a Hong Kong hospital as I write. She longs to put her affairs into order, but her daughter Helen stubbornly refuses to have anything to do with her grandmother's past. The surviving descendants of Yip Min-yuk's brother had to be informed so that they could take matters into their own hands and distribute what was left of the former fortune. This was the task I had been asked to perform and as a friend of the family I could not refuse.

It took much wandering and questioning until my companion and I arrived at a small village in a Guangzhou suburb. Astonished faces greeted us. The old man, his tiny wife, and two of his five sons, were putting the finishing touches to their second home. The peasants in this particular village are doing well. The eldest son was crouching on a wooden chair opposite me, facing the unexpected prosperity with calm and concentration. The old woman slipped out of the room having offered us hot water and shooed away curious village children, no doubt sent by their still more curious parents to enquire into the matter of the foreigner's visit. The eldest son discussed with his father the problem of bringing Hong Kong money across the border. Their faces were grave and the marvel at the strangers' presence forgotten temporarily.

The room, with its electric fan already wrapped up in acknowledgement of the summer's end, the sideboard bearing a large thermos-flask and six glasses on a tea-towel, a folding-table leaning against the wall, a long bench and assorted chairs, the high ceiling curving into the roof... imprinted themselves on my mind.

But on my way home I began to tell my companion the history of the women in Hong Kong and of the family we had just left, of my research in Hong Kong – and again I was vividly conscious of mother and daughter, still caught up within the time-span of pain.

Notes

Abbreviations: CM= China Mail; HKDP = Hong Kong Daily Press; HKWP & . . .
= Hong Kong Weekly Press & China Overland Trade Reports;
SCMP = South China Morning Post.

Threads: Introduction

1. Japanese occupation of Hong Kong effectively terminated British administration between 1941 and 1945, but many pre-1942 policies (e.g., those associated with trading in mooi-jai) were resumed after the occupation with diminished commitment, or not at all. The absence of comprehensive statistics on the presence of mooi-jai during and after the 1940s reflects this historical factor.

The official pre-1942 statistics concerning the registration of mooi-jai in Hong Kong were considered controversial and unreliable (see below).

Motifs

Moot Xiao-li

1. The re-creation of the lives of Moot Xiao-li and her descendants is based on several months of formal and informal interviewing. The latter became particularly important to me as the sharing of everyday tasks, daily exchanges about current events and reminiscences enabled me to observe the landscape of their visions and construct from it the context within which I would review the meaningfulness of their actions.

Information is based on interviews with Helen Chan (grand-daughter of Moot Xiao-li), Chan Kam-yang (daughter of Moot Xiao-li), and the Yeung sisters (grand-daughters of Meng Achoi, descended from his first wife).

2. Bento da Franca, 1897: 168–70.

3. I use the Cantonese term mooi-jai (mui-tsai) because that was how she came to be known in Hong Kong and South China where Moot Xiao-li and other mooi-jai lived. In colloquial speech it can carry two meanings: 'little sister' (rising tone) or 'little servant-girl' and 'slave girl' (high steady tone). The last meaning is the one used throughout the book.

4. *1921 Hong Kong Census Report.* Quoted in HKDP, 7 Dec. 1921: 3.

5. Mai Mei-sheng, 1933: 83–4. For interpretations of the meaning of cho-jue-fa, see Kani, H., 1979; vi, vii, 310.

6. This custom was especially popular among the Tanka boat-people; a little girl cost less than one-third of the price of a grown-up bride. Usually, around 16 years old a simple ceremony would mark her change in status from tung-yeung-sik to

wife. But not always, and the girl instead could be used as a life-long servant. Chen Xu-jing, 1946: 57.

7. *Mui Tsai Commission*, 1937. Vol. I: 239, PRO, London. For a single woman the fostering of a 'courtesy child' was common practice in Chinese society. As a form of quasi-adoption it allowed for the inheritance of property. See Leonard Pegg, 1979, 1980. This practice must be distinguished from the exploitation of girls for commercial gains, which had developed in response to a large market for girls in urban areas.

8. On the traditional use of these manuals, see Robert Van Gulik, 1951 and 1961.

9. One day in April 1978, I walked with my informant Helen Chan through the old part of Hong Kong Island to see some Buddhist nunneries and to visit a nunnery which kept her step-cousin's tablets of family ancestors. We were admitted by the Mother Superior to a humble temple. About six or seven young nuns with closely-shaven heads were present, but there were also small girls, obviously at home in their surroundings. My informant told me what seems common knowledge among Chinese, that these girls are bought when young (sometimes only 4 or 5 years old) from poor parents and raised by the nuns for the purpose of succession. These children are not there of their own free will and are more or less trapped for life. They are sent to school, but their freedom of movement is otherwise restricted. A relative of my informant paid a considerable sum to buy the freedom of one of these young novices.

10. *Mui Tsai Commission*, 1937. Minority Report: 238.

11. Chen Dongyuan, 1937: 208–9.

12. Widowers while in mourning could remarry, but were 'apt to be laughed at by their neighbours and friends' if they did so before the full year was up. See J. Doolittle, 1868: 159.

13. An unprecedented population explosion in the 18th and 19th century put great pressure on land and food resources:

Population of Guangdong 1787–1850

	1787	1812	1842	1850
Millions of people	16	19	26	28
Percentage increase	–	19%	36%	8%
Density per square mile	160	192	264	284
National median density per square mile	419	509	631	n/a
National mean density per square mile	256	278	349	n/a

Source: F. E. Wakeman, 1966: 179–80.
See also: A. H. Y. Lin, 1976; G. Smith, 1847: 49; and J. H. Gray, 1875: 185.

14. Carl T. Smith, 1975, 1977, 1977a. His biographies of former missionary college students tell of commercial rather than spiritual success – a problem that had preoccupied missionaries since the first schools were opened in China. Some said that acquisition of the English language granted vital access to Western civilization and Christianization, arguing that it contained conceptual tools not found in the Chinese language. Rev. H. V. Noyes, 1869: 249–55.

Not only did knowledge of the English language grant access to spiritual enlightenment, but also gave access to lucrative government and commercial positions; thus to the temptation to forsake the promise of a better life in another world with something more tangible in this world. See account of the lives of Hong Kong's early Chinese élite in Carl T. Smith, 1977c.

15. Carl T. Smith, 1975, divides élite Chinese in 19th century Hong Kong into five groups: contractors, merchants, compradors, government servants, and those who worked for the various missions.

16. Hao Yen-p'ing, 1970.

17. Ibid.

18. N. Cameron, 1978: 49. See also *CO 129/206*, file page: 165. Speaking to the deputation of the Aborigines Protection Society in London the Governor Sir John Pope Hennessy talked about changes that had occurred under his governorship in Hong Kong particularly concerning the position of Chinese there: when he went to Hong Kong in 1876, 12 of the principal 20 ratepayers were foreigners and eight Chinese. But in 1881, three of the principal 20 were foreigners and 17 Chinese; trade had improved greatly because of Chinese business acumen.

19. G. Smith, 1847: 82.

20. H. J. Lethbridge, 1971, 1972, 1972a; and A. K. N. Li, 1968: 639–42.

21. H. J. Lethbridge, 1972: 47.

22. J. Hayes, 1975: 4–5. For an official viewpoint of the Chinese élite involvement in the government of Hong Kong, see *CO 129/510/11*. File pages: 8–13.

23. The little existing information about Meng Achoi's origins had to be collated from wills, memorials, subscription lists, and the like (his family professes ignorance) and credit must go to Carl T. Smith's meticulous scholarship.

24. In 1877, English travellers commented on English merchants' use of pidgin-English when they gave orders to their Chinese clerks and compradors, as this 'silliest of baby-talk'; e.g., 'Take the lady's bag upstairs' became 'Take piecey missisy one piecy bag topside'. Their English acquaintances explained that this complex gibberish was 'easier to Chinaman's intellect'. A contemporary visitor wrote of pidgin-English as 'revolting'. 'The most dignified persons demean themselves by speaking it. How the whole English-speaking community, without distinction of rank, has come to communicate with the Chinese in this baby-talk is extraordinary.' James Pope-Hennessy, 1969: 69.

25. Meng's name first appeared publicly in 1852 when, in connection with a court case, he was listed in a newspaper as a lawyer's clerk.

26. For reference to Meng's growing fortune, see Carl T. Smith, 1975: 85–6.

27. Mention of Meng's appointment was made in the CM, 19 November 1883, and in the *Daily Press*, 3 December 1883.

28. In a list of names of Chinese JPs that appeared on 6 March 1903, in the HKWP, Meng's name does not appear. Considering that JP appointments were for life this fact introduces an element of doubt regarding Meng's continued status in Hong Kong's élite circles. So far I have no clue as to what might have happened to him in 1903.

29. The following data on Meng were provided by Carl T. Smith: *Hong Kong Recorder*, 19/10/1859: contributed HK$10, one of the largest individual contributions; signed in romanized script; 1864: presented a carved screen for Cleverly; 7/4/1880: contributed HK$100 to the Irish Disaster Fund; *Government Gazette*, 22/4/1881: name among the signatures to a Chinese petition on kidnapping; 22/4/1881: name on a memorial to Governor of Hong Kong on fourth anniversary of his arrival in Hong Kong; *CM*, 28/2/1882: present at banquet, Tung Wah Hospital, in honour of Governor Hennessy; 1/6/1883: present at the Government House ball, to celebrate Queen Victoria's birthday; 26/4/1887: gave public address; 20/5/1887: present at meeting of Chinese residents to decide on

suitable site for Chinese Chamber of Commerce; 24/6/1887: name appeared fifth on list of signatures on a memorial on public health; 3/4/1890: present when Chinese residents entertained the Duke and Duchess of Connaught; 20/10/1880: second on the list for a levee at the Government house; 1893: not on any list; 29/6/1897: name absent from published list of contributions to important Jubilee Fund; 31/10/1901: present at a dinner and entertainment for the Prince Chan; 1902: name absent from the Coronation Celebration Fund.

Tung Wah Hospital Directorships were important indicators of a man's social standing and influence in Hong Kong. One name mentioned in 1881 *could* be Meng Achoi, but it is mere speculation as the use of several names introduces the problem of identification. Smith thinks Meng Achoi could have been the individual as no one else would have fitted the bill.

This list is interesting for the light thrown on the individual Meng, and also in what it tells us about the public role-performance expected from a man who aspires to 'face', *mianzi*.

30. The daughter, Mrs Ko, and her great-niece. Interview June 1978.

31. Informant Chan Kam-yang.

32. Informants Chan Kam-yang and Mrs Ko.

33. Daughter and grand-daughter of Xiao-li differ greatly in how they perceive their ancestor's personality. The daughter, imbued with values transmitted to her by the mother, largely views the mother's life as one big success-story. The grand-daughter reacts strongly against a background of mutual exploitation and female degradation. Their different interpretations of past events were a constant feature throughout the months of interviewing.

34. Even Xiao-li's standing as a concubine was later to be contested by the daai-poh's descendants. In the 30 years of litigation, following Meng Achoi's death in 1911, Xiao-li's adversaries in the battle over the family fortune contended that she was a 'single woman' (e.g., her only link was by virtue of having rendered sexual services to Meng Achoi and this laid no other financial obligations on his family; she had been amply rewarded during Meng's lifetime). Here, disappointed heirs expressed 'violations of the rules of propriety' as it befitted benefactors of a patrilineal society, using this argument as an ideological weapon against the woman outsider.

35. Of the female focus in Chinese kinship, Margery Wolf says: 'Her irrelevance to her father's family may result in her having little reverence for descent lines, but she has warm memories of the security of the family her mother created. If she is ever to return to this certainty and sense of belonging, a woman must create her own uterine family by bearing children, a goal that happily corresponds to the goals of the family into which she has married.' Margery Wolf, 1972: 361.

'With a female focus, however, we see the Chinese family not as a continuous line stretching between the vague horizons of past and future, but as a contemporary group that comes into existence out of one woman's need and is held together insofar as she has the strength to do so, or, for that matter, the need to do so.' Ibid.: 37.

36. Margery Wolf describes the 'shutting out' from the natal home thus: 'The father or his representative hands the sedan chair bearers an *ang pau*, and the bearers lower the handles of the chair so the bride may enter. The chair is closed, and the bearers carry it out of the house. The house doors are quickly slammed behind the bride's chair to prevent the wealth of the family from following the bride. Her brother spits or throws water on the departing chair to indicate that just as spilt water cannot be returned to the container, so the bride cannot return to her natal

home – a thoroughly demoralizing statement, no matter how ritualized'. Ibid.: 136.

Where it did happen that the married daughter came back to her parents, she was received in shame – like a discarded commodity. Maxine Hong Kingston tells how a Chinese aunt was returned to her home, pregnant from an adulterous affair. At the night of giving birth, the village banded together and raided the house. 'My mother spoke about the raid as if she had seen it, when she and my aunt, a daughter-in-law to a different household, should not have been living together at all. Daughters-in-law lived with their husbands' parents, not their own; a synonym for marriage in Chinese is "taking a daughter-in-law". Her husband's parents could have sold her, mortgaged her, stoned her. But they had sent her back to her own mother and father, a mysterious act hinting at disgraces not told me. Perhaps they had thrown her out to deflect the avengers.' 1978: 7–8.

37. Regional variations and the social status of the women's natal family should, however, be kept in mind. Both factors qualified the control exercised by the husband's family over the daughter-in-law. See Maurice Freedman, 1965, (especially chs. 3 and 13); and 1966, ch. 2.

38. Interviews with Chan Kam-yang and her daughter Helen.

39. Interviews with Helen Chan and the Yeung sisters.

40. Ibid. Also C. S. Wong, 1967: 148, regarding the customary sacrifices to the moon: 'When the nocturnal orb is shining in all her brilliance, the senior members of the family, particularly members of the fair sex, make sacrificial offerings in the open air, usually on a terrace. Upon the open-air altar is placed a plate of moon-cakes. Besides the cakes, there are fruits like melons, pomelos, ground-nuts, yam (*keladi* or taro especially from China), water calthrops and cups of tea. The ceremony is accompanied by the customary lighting of joss-sticks and red candles and the burning of joss-papers of the gold-leaf variety ... At this ceremony, the cakes, fruits and nuts acquire a special significance, indicating the fullness of family life, vigour and youth, longevity, and numerous progeny. With other families, boxes of face-powder and cosmetics are also placed on the altar and after the prayers, these articles are believed to be endowed with the secret of beautifying the complexion. At the same time, the moon is invoked to bless the female devotees with handsome, robust and intelligent offspring'.

41. Chinese cosmology placed each individual in a unique relationship to the forces around them. Particular adversities in life could be suggestive of 'weak fate' preventing an individual gaining what was desirable in life. In the same way that certain ritual control could remedy 'weak fate' (see Marjorie Topley, 1967: 99–118) the possibility of influencing demons lent itself to abuse as in Kam-yang's case.

42. In Hong Kong many ritual healers were women. 'Some elderly women – often domestic servants or housewives – act as general consultants (for a small fee) and will perform ritual on behalf of clients. In fact many women one sees performing rites in Hong Kong are acting for payment on behalf of others. They usually have a broad general knowledge of occult matters – knowing for example the names and interests of various gods and habits of demons.' Marjorie Topley, 1967. On types of fu see ibid.: 110–11. For a more general discussion of Chinese ideas and concepts in terms of Great Tradition and Little Tradition, see Topley, 1967a: 7–21.

43. Every self-respecting Chinese who could afford to kept these garments in readiness for death.

44. Chan Kam-yang. This took place when her father had been dead for a number of years. *Mu-lan*, the famous female warrior, features both in literature and folklore. She donned male clothing to go to war on her father's behalf.

45. Whenever this statement was made, Helen would protest, demonstrating

instances of her grandmother's 'piety': the sale of her nieces, the trafficking in mooi-jai when Xiao-li was already a wealthy concubine.

46. Here one agrees with M. Topley who describes the attitude of Chinese towards systems of belief as utilitarian: one practises what had proved to be effective, 'if it works it is true'. Human beings create only the gods they know. Topley, 1967a: 19.

47. My experience in Hong Kong was that Chinese women of all classes would make use of a spirit-medium; regardless of their membership of a given church or sect, women saw the medium as fulfilling an indispensable ritual function.

48. Religious eclecticism is the hallmark of most Hong Kong Chinese families and becomes most visible in the education of their children. Jean Gittins tells of her family-life in Hong Kong before the War, that weddings were celebrated in Western style and funerals held in traditional Confucianist style. Her mother was a devout Buddhist but ancestral worship was strictly observed in their household. Daughters were sent to missionary schools and learnt the catechism under Western teachers. After their homework they studied the Confucianist classics with a private tutor. Gittins, 1969.

49. A fact that especially Helen Chan liked to emphasize whenever her mother talked of the 'economic necessity' which compelled Moot to sell his daughter.

50. Helen blames on her mother (and by implication her grandmother) the source of disorder and confusion that beset the family's history in her eyes. The threat she perceives for herself is the threat society has always attributed to persons in the social margin and to their polluting powers; thus Helen's daily obsession with cleansing acts that cannot be justified by objective necessity:

'Some pollutions are too grave for the offender to be allowed to survive. But most pollutions have a very simple remedy for undoing their effects. There are rites of reversing, untying, burying, washing, erasing, fumigating, and so on, which at a small cost of time and effort can satisfactorily expunge them. The cancelling of a moral offence depends on the state of mind of the offended party and on the sweetness of nursing revenge. The social consequences of some offences ripple out in all directions and can never be reversed'. Mary Douglas, 1976: 135–6.

Old To, the 'Xiang Fei'

51. Interviews with members of the To family and Lee family (parents of Old To's youngest son's wife); July and August 1978.

52. A. Bell, 1917: 67. Bell also reports (p. 68) that the largest opium factory he was shown on Macau paid the Portuguese government $1,560,000 each year in revenue. The opium was smuggled wholesale into China.

53. In 1905, J. Dyer Ball wrote that the barrier-wall dividing Macau from China was erected in 1573, 'for the protection of the country [China] and to prevent Chinese children from being kidnapped.' 1905: 5.

'Various attempts made by the church in Macau and by various colonial governments to stem the trafficking in girls proved ineffectual. The ever-present demand for concubines, entertainers, prostitutes and domestic drudges was met from a limitless supply of girls and women from impoverished rural areas in southern China.' Bento da Franca, 1987, 'A mulher China' in *Macau E Os Seus Habitantes*; see also Manuel Teixeira, 1965, in *Os Macaenses*.

54. Travelling was easy: the Hong Kong Canton and Macau Steamboat Company ran daily services between Hong Kong and Macau, Macau and Guangzhou, and Guangzhou and Hong Kong.

55. Xiang Fei; literally 'fragrant concubine'. *Xiang* had also the connotation of 'smelly' – fragrance turned by a wicked woman into 'smelliness' and 'dirtiness'. See Tsang Li-ho, 1938: 727, for a brief resumé of Xiang Fei's career and untimely death.

Margaret Leung's Grandmother

56. Wei Tao-ming listened as a young girl to her mother telling legends of the past: 'Of all of them the story of Mulan was her favourite and she never grew tired of hearing about her ... She described what the story of Mulan meant to her mother who was herself the daughter of a general and had led an unhappy life. As a young girl she had dreamed of freedom and happiness, all of which dreams had been frustrated. Physically timid and without education, she had suffered as a junior member of a large stifling household. The girl thought that since her mother was a victim of this and other facets of the system, "the story of Mulan is actually a projection of the dreams she held originally for herself and later gave to me".' (E. Croll, 1978: 34–5.)

Also, see Chiang Hsüeh-wen, in SINICA, XIV: 27–9.

57. During my fieldwork I met many Chinese women who were either the sole family breadwinner, or made substantial contributions to the family budget, and yet whose psychological dependence on men was not dissimilar from that of their house-bound mothers. Their perception of femaleness has yet to catch up with the change in their economic positions: the inversion of the history of Ibsen's Nora.

58. A simple presentation of Hong Kong statistics on educational facilities for girls has little value in itself. Availability of school facilities did not confer an automatic right to education for the average Chinese girl, even in urban areas; daughters of wealthy families were at a distinct advantage. (See Irene Cheng, *Lady Clara Ho* and Jean Gittins, *Eastern Windows – Western Skies*.) But even at this level a historian considering educational facilities before 1881 described these as very 'backward'. Few Government schools tended to admit girls. More common were mission schools where girls of upper-class families were taught by ladies. First beginnings were the founding of The Female Education Society in 1875 and the opening of the Government school for girls in 1890, with 34 pupils (G. B. Endacott, 1958: 238). By 1898 it had 539 pupils of whom nearly 50% (233 girls) were English. But an enquiry in 1883 found that only one-third of the registered children actually appeared at school (ibid.: 239). Girls in schools rose from 18% of pupils in 1880 to 32% in 1890 (ibid.: 240).

Yet in 1923 it was estimated that 90% of the Colony's Chinese population could neither read nor write (ibid.: 295). The poor rarely had time to send their children, particularly their daughters, to school. They were needed to look after their younger siblings at home, or help supplement the family's meagre income. It needed training for prostitution, as in the case of Margaret's father's concubine, to acquire rudimentary learning. But that school facilities for girls existed and flourished was of educational value to public opinion on female education – however slow in changing its conservative evaluation of a 'woman's place'.

In the years when Helen Chan and Margaret Leung went to school the intake of girl pupils had continued to show an upward trend:

Number of schools and scholars for the year 1936

Class of Institutions	Government Schools		Grant-in-Aid and Subsidized Schools		Unaided Schools	
	No. of Inst.	On Roll	No. of Inst.	On Roll	No. of Inst.	On Roll
English:-						
Secondary	4*	2,238	14	6,785	6	893
Primary	11**	1,843	2	243	115	4,695
Vocational	2	907	–	–	7	375
Total:	17	4,988	16†	7,028	128	5,963
Vernacular:-						
Secondary	1	247	4††	964	–	–
Primary	–	–	294	19,955	660	40,022
Vocational	2	211	–	–	1	301
Total:	3	458	298	20,919	661	40,323

Total Number of Institutions   1,123
Total on Roll   79,679

*   Out of four English secondary schools, there was one Anglo-Chinese School for girls and one mixed school.
**   Out of 11 English schools, three were mixed schools.
†   Eight schools were for girls
††   These were schools for girls.

Source: Administrative Reports. Hong Kong, 1936: 27–8.

59. See Carl T. Smith, 1977b and 1977.
60. Ban Zhao (Pan Chao) wrote in the first century AD; her classics *Nü Jie* and *Nü-er Jing* influenced notions of female propriety down to the 20th century. See E. Croll, 1978: 13–14.
61. Margaret Leung, interview.
62. These seven concubines were all taken from brothels. When I asked an informant why Leung chose prostitutes for concubines, she replied, 'Who would not prefer an iced sweet cake to an old hag.' Sexual experience was highly valued; provided a man did not actually marry a prostitute, what he did in his home did not matter.
63. Whenever the father had a new mistress he gave every prostitute in the brothel a great deal of money, 'To make everyone love and admire him. Then he felt happy'. He also participated in the party games of the rich: one game involved making congee on a fire fed with $500 notes.
64. Margaret Leung, interview.
65. She insisted she was a concubine. But against customary conventions she had never been part of the family and accepted as such by the daai-poh. On the contrary, hers was a rival household, with a separate identity, and not an affirmation of the identity of the main lineage.
66. Another upper-class Chinese informant, Margaret Hsu, told me that this used to be common in rich families. Her uncles and cousins would not have dreamt of looking at price-tags. This was the job of the servant, following closely behind.

67. Interview with the old woman, and with her friend, Chan Kam-yang.

68. See Margery Wolf, 1972.

69. See, for example, P. M. Yap, 1958: 75–8. He found that unlike Western countries the total rate of female suicide was more than half that of the male. In attempted suicide the number of females between 11 and 35 was higher than expected; for fatal acts of suicide the proportion of men was higher. In attempted suicide, single women were more numerous, and married less numerous, than might be expected. The divorcées and concubines showed the highest suicide rates; the married the lowest.

Suicidal acts were highest for, among others, prostitutes and entertainers; economic stress brought about more suicidal cases in men, interpersonal conflicts affected the number of women suicides.

70. Neither the independence of the Shunde women, nor the custom of female infanticide, were within the experience of many of my informants, but the memory of these was strong. As regards infanticide, the historian is faced with the lack of quantifiable data, and this clearly makes for a cautious approach to the reports presented by, for example, George Smith and John Henry Gray, both 19th century writers. However, this does not invalidate the strength of Chinese women's consciousness of their past – of which female infanticide was a most painful aspect. G. Smith, 1847, especially ch. 30; J. H. Gray, 1875/1974: 567–8. See also J. J. Matignon, 1899: 226.

71. For example, Margery Wolf, 1972.

72. It was their *being* rather than their *becoming* which marked their position in society, to use the phenomenological vocabulary of S. de Beauvoir, 1974.

73. See E. Ardener (ed.) 1975: xii, for a feminist anthropologist's perspective on the 'mutedness' of women.

Ma Xin's Mooi-Jai, Yuet-sim, Number Three Mooi

74. E. Ardener (ed.) 1975: 1–19.

75. See, for example, James L. Watson (ed.) 1980, where he argues that due to her essential outsider status in a system characterized by the male-dominated patrilineage, the female's position was flexible compared to the rigidity with which men were positioned in society. 'It was not impossible for a girl to be purchased as a daughter in infancy, exploited like a slave during adolescence, and married to one of her buyer's own sons in adulthood.' (p. 224).

The Tapestry

Hong Kong Society

1. See Appendix A for a comprehensive chronicle of the campaign to abolish the mooi-jai practice in Hong Kong.

2. *1880–1882. Alleged Existence of Chinese Slavery in Hong Kong.* HMSO. 1882.

3. See Sybille van der Sprenkel, 1962; and M. J. Meijer, 1979.

4. For example, Walter H. Mallory (1926: 2–3) said of the effects of the 1920/21 famine that 'the sale of women and children, particularly young girls, reached such proportions that a special Committee was organized for the protection of children.' For further discussion of the impact of natural calamities on women's lives see Li Yu-ning and Zhang Yufa (eds.) 1975, Vol.I: 65–6; and A. J. Nathan, 1965.

5. Stubbs to CO, London. Letter, 31 May 1921. *CO129/473.*

6. Eventually the Memorandum was printed in the *Eastern*, No. 137, November

1921; it was submitted to the CO on 27 June 1921. *CO129/473*.

7. See Noreen Branson, 1975.

8. HKDP. 28 October 1932: 543.

9. J. D. Bush, for the Anti-Mooi-Jai Society, in evidence to the Mui Tsai Commission stated that the mainly Chinese membership of the Society totalled 1,230. Most members came from the lower and middle classes, very few from upper-class or wealthy backgrounds. Mui Tsai Commission, 1937: I: 211–16. Also, see Appendix I., *Mui Tsai in Hong Kong and Malaya*. HMSO.

10. Occasionally, women sat on the Committee of the Anti-Mooi-Jai Society; in 1928 there were six women. See Appendix I., *Mui Tsai in Hong Kong and Malaya*. HMSO.

11. Mai Mei-sheng, 1933: 101.

12. The Society's constitution noted expressly that it did not represent partisan opinion and invited like-minded people irrespective of sex, nationality, religion or domicile to join the Society, whose object was 'to oppose the evil practice of rearing mui tsai, to assist the public to realize their mistake in continuing this practice, and to devise the best ways and means to effect abolition of the mui tsai system.' HKWP &..., 27 August 1921: 193.

The Transaction

13. This and the 'Mooi-Jai' section are based on the study of 228 mooi-jai cases, extracted from local Hong Kong papers and from enquiries conducted by various League of Nations Commissions and the 1937 Mui Tsai Commission. I have also included material from interviews with former mooi-jai and former employers of mooi-jai wherever appropriate.

14. 17 December 1921: 3, HKDP.

15. League of Nations, Report on *Slavery*, 1938: 96.

16. *Mui Tsai Commission*, 1937: I: 139.

17. League of Nations, 1932: 171, Report on *Slavery*.

18. Interviews with Helen Chan, Chan Kam-yang, the Yeung family, Margaret Leung.

19. Helen Chan, Chan Kam-yang, interviews.

20. Wong family, interviews.

21. In 1922, a correspondent denied the Southern Government's contention that slave-traffic was effectively abolished in law and practice. In the Guangdong borderland area, says the correspondent, girls in great numbers are taken across the border to be sold. Members of the government have slaves, if called by a different name, so how could the trafficking be controlled if even the law participated in it? HKDP, 29 March 1922: 2.

22. 6 August 1921: 132, HKWP &....

23. A. G. Fisher and H. J. Fisher, 1970.

24. 10 August, 1929, SCMP.

25. Hong Kong Society for the Protection of Children, *Annual Reports* HKWP &... 22 May 1931: 725–6; 24 December 1931: 962; 8 July 1932: 51–2; 10 May 1934: 711–13; 27 December 1935: 954–7.

26. Interviews: Wong, Lai and Ho families.

27. Interview, Miss Wei Mo-fung.

28. *Mui Tsai Commission*, 1937, I: 79–81.

29. 5 July 1929, HKPW &... By that time the Cantonese Government had proclaimed the mooi-jai system abolished. In 1927 regulations were issued for the emancipation of slaves and mooi-jai; paragraph 4 said: 'From the date of the

publication of these regulations, no girls shall be bought, sold or pledged as mui-tsai, and all agreements for such purposes shall be null and void' (League of Nations, 1932: 163, Annex III). The penal code of the Republic which entered into force on 1 September 1928 made such transactions unlawful, with article 313 stating explicitly that 'whoever forces a person into slavery shall be punishable by imprisonment for a term varying from one year to seven years. Attempt to commit the offence mentioned in the present article shall be punishable' (ibid.: 160–2). But as the League of Nations Committee rightly remarked in its criticism of the above legislation, as only the *sale* of children and females was prohibited, 'transfer of paternal authority' could still legitimately be claimed.

30. League of Nations, 1932: 138. A Shanghai official's statement.

31. The bao-fan, especially widespread in Shanghai cotton mills, was a contract labour system that bound female labourers to a middle-man who was responsible to the girl's employer for her performance at work. Often he might have several of them. The contractor paid a small sum of money to parents (in the rural areas) in return for appropriation of the girl's wages over a defined period of years. He was responsible for her person and might or might not give her a little pocket-money. 'Girls are "non-free" in the sense that they are beholden, that they are closely supervised going to and from their work, and have little personal liberty.' (*League of Nations Report*, 1938: 97). Parents of girls under labour contract might be paid $30 to $40.

32. The families of Lai, Wong, Lee, Leung, Ho; interviews.

33. It was maintained that taking a girl involved a *personal* obligation and legal documents would have been regarded as a kind of insult; none of the mooi-jai kept by these families retained contact with their natal families. The gist of this was that with everything they could wish for, why should they stay in contact with a family which could provide them with nothing, and had, in fact, sold them?

The girl's name was usually changed to Yat Mooi or Saam Mooi (No. One or No. Three mooi) but this was never regarded as a ritual of adoption. The mooi-jai's close link with the master's family was stressed, but whenever I asked directly if this was like being a daughter, it was emphatically denied. 'No, she was not like a daughter, more like a helper' (Mr Wong).

34. When rich men's daughters were 6 years old, they often received as a present a 9-year-old mooi, luk gau mooi, who, according to the ancient custom, was to bring luck to the young mistress. This mooi accompanied the young mistress and served her personally, often for a life-time (see above).

35. Wong, interviews.

36. Teaching mooi-jai was often regarded as charitable work, once they became a social issue in Hong Kong. Thus Chan Kam-yang taught classes of mooi-jai reading and writing.

37. Helen Chan, Chan Kam-yang and Ho family, interviews. In his article on slavery in China before 1910 (the year of abolition) Meijer refers to the frequent cruelty with which women of official households treated their slave-girls: 'Cruel treatment of slave girls by the lady of the house seems to have been especially frequent among officials, and rare among slave-owning commoners. These titled ladies would invoke their status in order to escape punishment. Once during the reign of the Tung-chih emperor (1861–75) a censor, enraged at the impunity with which such women could vent their sadistic inclinations on their slave girls, wanted to hold the official himself responsible. The Board of Punishment sympathized with the censor's intentions (respect for human life) but at the same time wished to maintain the social distinction and proposed a compromise' M. J. Meijer, 1979.

126 Concubines and Bondservants

38. See J. Lim, 1958, for an account of serving in a household with children.
39. Lee family, interviews.
40. Lee, Ho, Wong, interviews.
41. I was shown wills in which mistresses had left their companions considerable amounts of money, more than would be justified by however long a service. Interviewees maintained that such physical relationships 'were quite common'.
42. Ho family and Helen Chan, interviews.
43. ILO-China branch reports to Geneva, covering practically the whole of the 1930s, provide a comprehensive analysis of economic and social conditions in China as a whole. *ILO-Archive*, especially the file-series *C 1802* and *C 1803*, Geneva.
44. Aline Lai-chung Kan, 1971: 104.
45. Helen Chan, interview.
46. 8 February 1921: 3, HKDP.
47. Lai Chin-hing, interview, March 1978, Hong Kong. She was born in China, the last daughter of a rich family. Her home at times employed 30 mooi-jai. After the war she came to Hong Kong with her closest and favourite mooi-jai and let her marry a farmer at the age of 26 years. She was interviewed on two occasions.
48. April 1930: 592, HKWP &....
49. 25 January 1921: 3, HKDP.
50. Communication by the Anti-Mooi-Jai Society, 20 March 1929, to the Secretary for Chinese Affairs, R. A. C. North. *CO 129/516/7*. File-page: 57.

Mooi-jai
51. Consul at Amoy, W. Russell Brown, in a letter to the Governor of Hong Kong, C. Clementi. *Sessional Papers before the Legislative Council of Hong Kong*, 1929: 250. (Letter, 1 May 1929.)
52. 6 July 1975, SCMP, article by Lucy Ching. The mooi-jai, Ah Yung, was presented to Lucy Ching's family by her sixth uncle as a gesture of gratitude for past financial support. The uncle showed the contract, signed by Ah Yung's parents, disclaiming all rights in their daughter's future and granting the buyer the right to employ, marry off, or give her away, as he pleased.
53. Helen Chan, personal communication, November 1978.
54. Ibid.
55. 25 November 1932: 717, HKWP &....
56. Miss Wei Mo-fung, interview.
57. 19 July 1929: 79, HKWP &....
58. *Mui Tsai Commission, 1937*, I: 10–11.
59. Ibid.: 78.
60. 8 June 1933: 32, HKWP &....
61. Tsoi Lan and Sui Ning, former mooi-jai, interviews.
62. *Mui Tsai Commission 1937*.
63. Lee family and Wong family interviews.
64. *Mui Tsai Commission, 1937*, I: 60.
65. Ibid.: 58.
66. Ibid.: Minority report: 219.
67. The estimate of 12,000 must still be considered very conservative, as the heavy influx of refugees was never adequately monitored in Hong Kong.
68. Tsoi Lan and Sui Ning, interviews.
69. *Mui Tsai Commission*, 1937, I: 61.
70. *Mui Tsai in Hong Kong, 1935*. Committee appointed by Sir John Peel. HMSO. London.

71. See Motifs.

72. *CO 129/516/7*. File page: 56.

73. League of Nations, *Slavery*, 1932: 476–87

74. Tsoi Lan and Sui Ning, interviews.

75. 17 April 1930: 568, HKWP & ....

76. 28 December 1922, WKYP, Wai Fung, 'My opinion on the protection of slave girls'.

77. From Mai Mei-sheng, 1933: 315–88.

78. 8 February 1921: 3, HKDP, medical evidence given at the trial.

79. 8 June 1921: 3, HKDP.

80. J. J. M. De Groot, reprint 1964: 546.

81. Arthur P. Wolf, 1970: 196.

82. De Groot, 1964: 513.

83. M. Freedman, 1965: 4.

84. For a description of funerary rites for an unmarried youth, girl or boy, see J. G. Cormack, 1927: 66–7.

85. Expert Opinion given by Dr S. W. Ts'o, Chinese member of the Hong Kong Legislative Council, in a mooi-jai case tried on 26 September 1929. *Sessional Papers laid before the Legislative Council of Hong Kong*. 1928: 255–6.

86. Maurice Freedman, 1957: 57.

87. Mai Mei-sheng, 1933: 317–18.

88. 13 March 1922: 3, HKDP.

Bibliography

Abbreviations used

HKBRAS   = Hong Kong Branch of the Royal Asiatic Society
SCMP   = South China Morning Post
HKWP   = Hong Kong Weekly Press & China Overland Trade Report.

(Details of government publications and of publications issued by non-governmental organizations appear in the *Notes*.)

Ahern, E. M. (1975) 'The Power and Pollution of Chinese Women' in M. J. Wolf & R. Witke (ed.) *Women in Chinese Society*. Stanford University Press.

Ardener, E. (ed.) (1975) *Perceiving Women*. London.

Arlington, L. C. (1931) *Through the Dragon's Eyes*. London.

Ba Jin (1977) *Jia*. Originally published in 1931. Beijing.

Bell, A. (1917) *The Spell of China*. Boston.

Benedict, R. (1971) *Patterns of Culture*. London.

Benson, S. (1925) *The Little World*. London.

Bernard, W. D. (1844) *Narrative of the Voyages and Services of The Nemesis, from 1840 to 1843*. 2 vols. London.

Branson, N. (1975) in *Britain in the Nineteen Twenties: The History of British Society*. (ed.) E. J. Hobsbawm. London.

Butters, H. R. (1939) *On Labour and Labour Conditions in Hong Kong*. Hong Kong.

Cameron, N. (1978) *Hong Kong. The Cultured Pearl*. Oxford University Press.

Chen Dongyuan (1937) *Zhongguo funü shenghuo shi*. Zhongguo wenhua congshu series.

Chen Xujing (1946) *Dan-minde yan-jiu*. Shanghai.

Cheng, I. (1976) *Clara Ho Tung: A Hong Kong Lady, Her Family and Her Times*. The Chinese University of Hong Kong.

Chesneaux, J. (1962) *Le Mouvement ouvrier chinois, de 1919 à 1927*. Paris.

Chiang Hsueh-wen (n.d.) 'Hua Mu Lan. Eine Amazone aus der Zeit der Tang-Dynastie' in SINICA, XIV. Heft 1/2. China Institut Frankfurt A.M.

Collins, C. (1952) *Public Administration in Hong Kong*. Royal Institute of International Affairs. London.

Collis, M. (1966) *Foreign Mud*. London.

Cormack, J. G. (1927) *Chinese Birthday, Wedding, Funeral, and other Customs*. China Booksellers Ltd. Peking.

Croll, E. (1978) *Feminism and Socialism in China*. London.

Da Franca, Bento (1897) 'A mulher china' in *Macau E Os Seus Habitantes*. Lisbon.

Dafydd, M. E. Evans (1975) 'The Foundation of Hong Kong: a Chapter of Accidents' in E. M. Topley (ed.) *Hong Kong: The Interactions of Traditions and Life in the Towns*. HKBRAS.

De Beauvoir, S. (1974) *The Second Sex*. Penguin, Harmondsworth.

De Groot, J. J. M. (1964) *The Religious System of China*. Taipei.

Doggett, J. (1970) *The Yip Family of Amah Rock*. Standard – Sing Tao Printer, Hong Kong.

Doolittle, J. (1868) *Social Life of the Chinese*. London.

Douglas, M. (1976) *Purity and Danger: An Analysis of Concepts of Pollution and Taboo*. Routledge & Kegan Paul.

Dyer Ball, J. (1905) *Macao: The Holy City: The Gem of the Orient Earth*. The China Baptist Publication Society. London.

———— (1925) *Things Chinese*. Hong Kong.

Eitel, E. J. (1895) *Europe in China*. Hong Kong.

Elliott, E. (1975) *The Traffic in Persons, The System in Hongkong*. Annexe E. Anti-Slavery Society for the Protection of Human Rights. London.

Endacott, G. B. (1958) *A History of Hong Kong*. Oxford University Press.

———— (1962) *A Biographical Sketch-book of Early Hong Kong*. Singapore.

Fisher, A. G. & Fisher, H. J. (1970) *Slavery and Muslim Society in Africa*. London.

Forster, L. (1933) *Echoes of Hong Kong and Beyond*. Hong Kong.

Freedman, M. (1957) *Chinese Family and Marriage in Singapore*. Colonial Research Study No. 20. HMSO, London.

———— (1965) *Lineage Organization in Southeastern China*. LSE Monographs on Social Anthropology. London.

———— (1966) *Chinese Lineage and Society: Fukien and Kwangtung*. LSE Monographs on Social Anthropology. London.

Gittings, J. (1973) *A Chinese View of China*. New York.

Gittins, J. (1969) *Eastern Windows – Western Skies*. SCMP Ltd. Hong Kong.

Gray, J. H. (1875) *Walks in the City of Canton*. Reprinted 1974. San Francisco.

Guo Moruo (1954) *Nuli shi shidai*. Beijing.

Hao Yen-p'ing (1970) *The Compradore in Nineteenth Century China: Bridge between East and West*. Harvard University Press.

Haslewood, Lieutenant & Mrs (1930) *Child Slavery in Hong Kong*. Anti-Slavery Society. London.

Hayes, J. (1975) 'Hong Kong: Tale of Two Cities' in HKBRAS.

———— (1977) *The Hongkong Region, 1850–1911: Institutions and Leadership in Town and Countryside*. Archon Books, Dawson.

Hinder, E. (1944) *Life and Labour in Shanghai*. Shanghai.

Hinton, W. (1972) *Fan-shen*. Pelican book.

Ho, D. Y. F. (1974) 'Face, Social Expectations, and Conflict Avoidance' in J. L. M. Dawson and W. J. Lonner (eds.) *Cross-Cultural Psychology*. Hong Kong University Press.

Hobsbawm, E. J. (ed.) (n.d.) *Britain in the Nineteen Twenties: The History of British Society*. London.

Hong Kingston, M. (1978) *The Woman Warrior: Memoirs of a Girlhood among Ghosts*. Penguin. Harmondsworth.

Ho Ping-ti (1967) *The Ladder of Success in Imperial China*. Columbia University Press. New York.

Ingrams, H. (1952) *Hong Kong*. HMSO. London.

Kan, Aline Lai-chung (1971) *The Kaifong (Neighbourhood) Associations in Hong Kong*. Ph.D. thesis, University of California, Berkeley. University microfilms.

Ann Arbor, Michigan.

Kani, H. (1979) *Kindai Chugoku no Kuri to* [*Chokka*]. Iwanami Shoten. Tokyo.

Kaplan, E. H. (transl.) (1971) *Maxims for the Well-Governed Household* by Chu Yung-ch'un. Western Washington. State College Program in East Asian Studies. Occasional Paper No. 1.

Lethbridge, H. J. (1971) 'The District Watch Committee: The Chinese Executive Council of Hong Kong' in HKBRAS.

———— (1972) 'The Evolution of a Chinese Voluntary Association in Hong Kong: The Po Leung Kuk' in *Journal of Oriental Studies*. Vol. X. No. 1.

———— (1972a) 'A Chinese Association in Hong Kong: the Tung Wah' in *Contributions to Asian Studies*. Vol. 1.

———— (1975) 'Caste, Class and Race in Hong Kong Before the Japanese Occupation' in M. Topley (ed.) *Hong Kong: Interactions of Tradition and Life in the Towns*.

———— (1978) *Hong Kong: Stability and Change*. Oxford University Press. Hong Kong.

Levy, H. S. (1966) *A Feast of Mist and Flowers. The Gay Quarters of Nanking at the End of the Ming*. Yokohama. Japan.

Li, A. K. N. (September 1968) 'Girls without Love' in *Far Eastern Economic Review*. Vol. LXI, No. 39.

Li Chien-nung (1967) *The Political History of China, 1840–1928*. Stanford University Press.

Li Wen-zhi (ed.) (1957) *Zhongguo jindai nongyehshi ziliao*. Beijing.

Li Yu-ning, Zhang Yu-fa (eds.) (1975) *Jindai Zhongguo nüguan yundong shiliao*. Vol. I. Harvard-Yenching Institute, Taipei.

Lim, J. (1958) *Sold for Silver: An Autobiography*. Collins, London.

Lin, A. H. Y. (1976) 'The Kwangtung Peasant Economy, 1875—1937. A Case Study of Rural Dislocation in Modern China'. Unpublished Ph.D. thesis. University of London, SOAS, Department of History.

Lo Hsiang-lin (1963) *Hong Kong and its External Communications Before 1842*. Institute of Chinese Culture. Hong Kong.

Lockwood, Stephen Chapman (1971) *Augustine Heard and Company, 1858–1862*. East Asian Research Center, Harvard University, Cambridge, Mass.

Mai Mei-sheng (1933) *Fandui xubi shilüe*. Hong Kong.

Mallory, W. H. (1926) *China: Land of Famine*. American Geographical Society. New York.

Marx, K. (1974 edition) *Capital*. Vol. I. Lawrence and Wishart. London.

Matignon, J. J. (1899) *Superstition, Crime et Misère en Chine*. Lyon.

McLeavy, H. (1959) *That Chinese Woman*. London.

Mead, M. and R. Métraux (eds.) (1953) *The Study of Culture at a Distance*. The University of Chicago Press.

Meijer, M. J. (1979) 'Slavery at the End of the Ch'ing Dynasty' in J. A. Cohen, F. M. Ch'en and R. Edwards (eds.) *China's Legal Tradition*. Princeton University Press.

Nathan, A. J. (1965) *A History of the China International Famine Relief Commission*. Harvard East Asian Monographs. Cambridge, Mass.

Noyes, H. V. (1869) 'On Teaching English to Chinese Assistants' in *The Chinese Recorder and Missionary Journal*. Vol. I, No. 12.

Pegg, L. (1979 and 1980) 'Children in the Family Law of Hong Kong' in *Hong Kong Law Journal*. No. 9 and No. 10.

Pippon, T. (1936) *Beitrag zum chinesischen Sklavensystem. Eine juristisch-*

soziologische Darstellung. Mitteilungen der Deutschen Gesellschaft für Natur- und Völkerkunde Ostasiens. Bd. XXIX.B.1405.

Pope-Hennessy, J. (1969) *Half Crown Colony.* London.

Pruitt, I. (1945) *A Daughter of Han.* The Autobiography of a Chinese Working Woman. Yale University Press.

————— (1979) *Old Madam Yin.* Stanford University Press.

Purcell, V. (1967) *The Chinese in Malaya.* Oxford University Press.

Sayer, G. R. (1937) *Hong Kong.* Oxford University Press.

Shi Xing (1973) *Nuli Shehui.* Shanghai.

Smedley, A. (1930) 'Kindersklaverei in Hong Kong' in *Frankfurter Zeitung,* 10 September.

Smith, Carl T. (1975) 'English-Educated Chinese Elites in Nineteenth-century Hong Kong' in HKBRAS.

————— (1977) 'Chan Lai-Sun and his Family: A 19th Century China Coast Family' in HKBRAS.

————— (1977a) 'The Early Hongkong Church and Traditional Chinese Family Patterns' in *Ching Feng.* Vol. XX, No. 1. Chinese University of Hong Kong.

————— (1977b) 'A Sense of History' in SCMP. Hong Kong.

Smith, G. (1847) *A Narrative of an Exploratory Visit to each of the Consular Cities of China.* London.

————— (1852) *A Letter to the Archbishop of Canterbury.* Hong Kong.

Teixeira, M. (1965) 'As Muitsai' in *Os Macaenses.* Centro de Informaçao E Turismo, Macau.

Topley, M. (1967) 'Is Confucius Dead?' in *Far Eastern Economic Review.* Vol. LVIII. No. 12.

————— (1967) 'Some Basic Conceptions and their Traditional Relationship to Society' in HKBRAS.

————— (1967a) 'Chinese Occasional Rites in Hong Kong' in HKBRAS.

Tsang Li-ho (ed.) (1938) *Chung-kuo jen-ming ta tz'u-tien.*

Van der Sprenkel, S. (1962) *Legal Institutions in Manchu China.* The Athlone Press. London.

Van Gulik, R. H. (1951) *Erotic Colour Prints of the Ming Period.* Privately published. Tokyo.

————— (1961) *Sexual Life in Ancient China.* Leiden.

Wakeman, F. E. (1966) *Strangers at the Gate: Social Disorder in Southern China, 1839-1861.* University of California Press.

Waley, A. (1958) *The Opium War Through Chinese Eyes.* London.

Wang Shu-nu (1935) *Zhongguo changji shi.* Shanghai.

Watson, J. L. (1980) 'Slavery as an Institution, Open and Closed Systems' in J. L. Watson (ed.) *Asian and African Systems of Slavery.* Basil Blackwell, Oxford.

Wei Tao-ming (1943) *My Revolutionary Years.* New York.

Wingfield, L. (1889) *Wanderings of a Globe-Trotter in the Far East.* 2 vols. London.

Wolf, A. P. (1970) 'Chinese Kinship and Mourning Dress' in M. Freedman (ed.) in *Family and Kinship in Chinese Society.* Stanford University Press.

————— (ed.) (1978) *Studies in Chinese Society.* Stanford University Press.

Wolf, M. (1972) *Women and the Family in Rural Taiwan.* Stanford University Press.

Wong, C. S. (1967) *A Cycle of Chinese Festivities.* Malaysia Publishing House Ltd., Singapore.

Xie Guozhen (1934) *Ming Qing zhi ji dangshe yundong kao.* Commercial Press. Shanghai.

Xu Lun (1964) *Shenma shi nuli zhidu.* Renmin chubanshe. Shanghai.

Yang, C. K. (1974) *Chinese Communist Society: The Family and the Village.* The MIT Press.

Yap, P. M. (1958) *Suicide in Hong Kong: with Special Reference to Attempted Suicide.* Hong Kong University Press.

Zhang Jingxian (1974) *Zhongguo nuli shehui.* Lishi zhishi duwu. Beijing.

Zhao Fengjie (1973) *Zhongguo funü zai falüshang zhi diwei.* Facsimile of the 1927 edition. Taipei.

Archives consulted

Anti-Slavery Society, Rhodes Library, Oxford.
ILO, Geneva.
League of Nations, Geneva.
PRO (Colonial Office-files), Hong Kong and London.
YWCA, Geneva.

Main informants

For *Moot Xiao-li*: Chan Kam-yang (daughter); Helen Chan (grand-daughter); and (descendants of Meng Achoi's first wife) Mrs Ko & the Yeung sisters.

For *Old To*: Lee Kun (daughter-in-law); Mr and Mrs Lee (Kun's parents); daughters of the merchant To's first wife.

For *Margaret Leung's Grandmother*: Margaret Leung (grand-daughter); Chan Kam-yang (friend of Leung family); Helen Chan (Margaret's schoolfriend); Margaret's teacher.

For *Ma Xin's Mooi-jai, Yuet-sim, Number Three Mooi*: Ma Xin (former mistress of mooi-jai); Yuet-Sim; Yuet-Sim's former master, Mr Yeo; Number Three Mooi; Number Three's former master, Mr Lai.

Mr Lai, mediation officer in the Secretariat of Chinese Affairs from 1951 to 1973. Miss Wei Mo-fung, former lady inspector of mooi-jai in the Secretariat of Chinese Affairs.

Appendixes

Appendix A: Chronology of Anti-Mooi-Jai Campaign, 1841-1938

1841: Upon taking possession of the island Captain C. Elliot proclaimed that the Chief Magistrate was authorized and required 'to exercise authority, according to the laws, customs, and usages of China, as near as may be (every description of torture excepted), for the preservation of the peace and the protection of life and property, over all the native inhabitants in the said island and the harbours thereof' and over other persons according to British law.[1]

1844: On 28 February the new Legislative Council of Hong Kong passed No. 1 Ordinance against the practice of slavery within the Colony. The Ordinance was disallowed and by proclamation of 24 January 1845, Queen Victoria promised and undertook that English law against slavery must be enforced by all Her Majesty's officers (civil and military) within the Colony.

1865: The Hong Kong Legislative Council passed the Offences Against the Person Ordinance, No. 2, prohibiting any form of sale of a human being, or his/her being held to ransom, or enticing a child away from its legal guardian.

1878: The Po Leung Kuk was founded when a group of leading Chinese sent a memorandum to the Governor of Hong Kong, Sir John Pope Hennessy, lamenting the prevalence of kidnapping of women and children in the Colony.

As Colonial Office (CO) minutes noted, the petition attacked the sale of females for prostitution, but resisted interference 'with the buying and selling of children for adoption or domestic service'.[2]

1879: During the Supreme Court Criminal Sessions in September, Chief Justice Sir John Smale made a judicial declaration when passing judgement on three cases involving trafficking in children: that two classes of slavery existed in the Colony: 1) domestic; and 2) for the purpose of prostitution.[3]

In this widely quoted and influential declaration the Chief Justice alleged that a widespread system of trafficking in the Colony existed, with slaves numbering around 10,000. He accused Government officials of turning a blind eye to slavery, considering it 'impolitic' to interfere. He reaffirmed that slavery in Hong Kong was absolutely illegal by force of law (Ordinances 6: 1845; and 12: 1873). Captain Elliot's 1841 proclamation did not include toleration of Chinese customs comparable with, or tantamount to, slavery.[4]

Sir John Smale reiterated that in Hong Kong the Common Law of England applied, as slavery could be introduced only by positive law, '... that no one can acquire any right over the person of another, that no man can sell his own person into slavery, that a parent has no saleable property in his child; moreover, that every such sale is *nudum pactum*, absolutely void, that money paid on any such sale cannot be recorded back; but that the man bought must be restored to liberty, and the sold child to his parent, and that the crime in buyer and seller must be punished'.[5]

On 6 October, Sir John Smale stated publicly from the Bench that slavery existed in the Colony and traffic in women and children was increasing.

1880-82: Despatches between Hong Kong and the CO followed in the wake of the Chief Justice's statements. These examined the evidence presented by Sir John and by the Government of Hong Kong through the Acting Chinese Secretary, Dr Eitel, whose influential report insisted that the alleged existence of slavery was in reality part of the peculiar social organism and national character of Chinese. He argued in essence that Chinese domestic servitude was peculiar and different from Negro slavery and could not be brought under the provisions of English enactments regarding slavery.

Secondly, Chinese domestic servitude had to be judged by the standards of Chinese civilization, founded on entirely different principles. Condemnation of such practice would be an act of moral injustice. Thirdly, Chinese domestic servitude constituted a necessary part of the social order and characterized the social life of Chinese residents in Hong Kong. To prohibit Chinese domestic servitude *in toto* constituted an act of violence. It would harm the Chinese social organism and be embarrassing to the British Government. Fourthly, the laws of evolution would eventually dissolve this custom along with the whole patriarchal organism. It would be unwise to interfere with this process.[6]

A final despatch from the Earl of Kimberley to the Governor of Hong Kong (18 March 1882) showed the influence of Dr Eitel's report. The Colonial Secretary of State concluded that Sir John Smale had been 'misled' by terms such as 'purchase' and 'sale' as in the Chinese context they allowed for different interpretations far removed from slavery. Whatever abuses did occur could be met by existing legislation.

Yet a modicum of doubt remained, '. . . the sellers have believed they have validly sold, and the buyers, that they have validly bought that for which money has passed, and the children themselves can scarcely help believing that they are in bond to their possessors.' Finally, admitting the evidence presented somewhat 'perplexing', he asked to 'institute a full and trustworthy inquiry into the facts', so that any 'evils' brought to light might be dealt with.[7]

1887: The Puisne Judge of Hong Kong, G. Russell, completed his 'Report on Child Adoption and Domestic Service among Hong Kong Chinese' (18 July 1886) and presented his report to the Legislative Council on 7 January 1887. The report took cognizance of the fact that perceptions of what constituted slavery were subject to cultural prejudices. It brought a critical eye to bear upon the discrepancy between what was said existed, and why it existed, and what took place in the twilight areas of society. Its conclusions were that, in contrast to male adoption, female adoption was rare and frequently a concealment of relationship of 'pocket-mother' with her 'pocket-daughter'.[8]

In the majority of cases 'Deeds of Sale' entailed bondage without redemption for the victim. (See above.) Obligations derived from Chinese custom upon purchasers of servants were enforced only by social sanction. By implication, these safeguards were precarious. Even where Hong Kong afforded legal protection, young girls instilled with the idea of total control over them by the 'pocket-mother' were not likely to put up much fight 'even if they knew all their rights'.[9]

Frequent crimes of kidnapping, fed on institutions of 'adopted daughter' or 'domestic servitude', brought forth lucrative transactions. As the number of 'adopted daughters' and 'domestic servants' in bondage could not be established Russell suggested a tightening up of regulations, much more selective power of supervision by the Registrar General over suspect persons, with a consulting Chinese Committee from the Po Leung Kuk. Otherwise, supervision in Hong Kong of prostitution was adequate and highly satisfactory.

1887: An Ordinance for the Better Protection of Young Girls provided that legal guardianship of girls must be invested in the Secretary for Chinese Affairs (formerly Registrar General).

1893: The Po Leung Kuk Incorporation Ordinance No. 6 was passed.

1897: The Protection of Women and Girls Ordinance was passed.

1915: The Asiatic Emigration Ordinance No. 30 of 1915 was passed. It extended protection to vulnerable Chinese women and children emigrants to Malaya or the East Indies from, or through, Hong Kong.

1917: The Boarding House Ordinance No. 23 was passed, which gave the licensing authority special powers of control over Boarding Houses which act as collecting or transit centres for women and juvenile emigrants. The Member of Parliament for Labour, Colonel Ward, visited Hong Kong where he stayed in command of a regiment at the local garrison. He became subsequently involved with the movement in London to abolish the mooi-jai custom.

On 23 August, a case of kidnapping was brought before the Chief Justice of Hong Kong. The defence lawyer, Mr Alabaster, 'caused a mild sensation' in the Court, when he pleaded not guilty on a legal point: that of 'unlawfully taking away two female children with intent to deprive two persons having lawful care and possesssion of such children.' Through cross-examination Mr Alabaster established the status of the girls to be that of slaves. As slavery was illegal in Hong Kong the right of possession over the children and resultant legal implications could not be upheld by the 'guardians'. This argument was not put to the test in the Court; but in his summing up the Chief Justice stressed that Chinese customs must not be interfered with. It was well-known that buying servants was an old Chinese practice in respect of which Captain Elliot's proclamation had expressly guaranteed inviolability.[10] Extensive press coverage gave evidence of the great public interest in the case.

1919: On 4 November, several papers published an open letter from Mrs C. B. L. Haslewood, wife of a naval officer stationed in Hong Kong, in which she proclaimed the existence of child slavery under the British flag and the need to remove this scourge from Hong Kong – if necessary by mobilizing the British Parliament at home.[11]

The Haslewood couple became two of the most passionate campaigners on behalf of mooi-jai – to the great exasperation of the CO, as CO files amply illustrate.[12]

Having been warned by the Governor to cease agitation, the couple moved to London and, with the close involvement of the Anti-Slavery Society, campaigned against official indifference and bureaucratic cynicism. The CO in turn treated them warily and with barely suppressed incivility. It was hoped in official circles in Hong Kong and London that they would face but 'a storm in the tea-cup', but the House of Commons and the press in London and Hong Kong soon became a forum for a wider debate not only of the mooi-jai custom, but also of the state of factory legislation (non-existent) and of child labour in Hong Kong.

1920: On 21 December a confidential despatch from the Governor of Hong Kong, Sir R. E. Stubbs, to the CO stated the position of his Government; that existing legislation and available Chinese welfare institutions were more than adequate to deal with cases of abuse of mooi-jai. On no account must the feelings of 'prominent Chinese' be hurt. Their reaction to educational opportunities for girls (if still nominal in comparison with those available to boys) was telling, as the Governor wrote: '. . . the overswing of the pendulum, shewn in the growth of private schools (of which there are many) is watched with some suspicion by responsible Chinese. In nine years they have lost a great part of their centuries-old control of their own women-kind, and fear to assist too much in the movement for the emancipation and independence of the new generation, to which they attribute at least some of the evils which now surround the problem.'[13]

1921: On 31 July the first mass meeting of Chinese took place in Hong Kong to discuss the mooi-jai controversy, resulting in the formation of the Society for the Prevention of Cruelty to Mooi-Jai under the conservative leadership of Mr Lau Chu-pak and Mr Ho Fook.

On 8 August the Anti-Mooi-Jai Society was formed, called into being in opposition to the Society sponsored by traditionalists. It opposed ' the evil practice of rearing mui tsai' and sought to devise 'the best ways and means to effect abolition of the mui tsai system'.[14] Mr J. M. Wong was elected Chairman, Dr Yeung was elected Vice-chairman. Mrs Ma joined the Committee as its only female member. Pressures on the CO to act were mounting. Prominent individuals, such as Lady Gladstone, accredited to the League of Nations, exhorted the CO to act before 'we are held up to shame before the world',[15] and contributed to its increasingly defensive position. The League of Nations sent out questionnaires in connection with the Traffic in Women and Children Report that bore heavily and embarrassingly on the mooi-jai question.[16]

On 27 June the Secretary for Chinese Affairs submitted his report on the question of mooi-jai. Soon the weakness of the Halifax report became apparent in that it did not deal with re-sale of a mooi-jai, the most problematic aspect of the practice.

1922: On 21 February the Under-Secretary of State for the Colonies under the Conservative Government, Mr Winston Churchill, wrote to Sir J. Masterton Smith: 'I am not prepared to go on defending this thing. Ask that all these questions [see below] should be put off for a week in order that I may make a comprehensive reply after receiving full reports I am calling for. Put to the Governor my intention to state that no compulsion of any kind will be allowed to prevent these persons from freely quitting their employment at any time they like.

I do not care a rap what the local consequences are. I am not going on defending it. You had better make it perfectly clear.'[17]

Mr Churchill had referred to questions put down by the MPs, Mr T. Richardson, Mr Edwards, Col Ward and Mr Griffith, for 28 February. On 22 February they were asked to postpone their questions for a week.

The tone of the cable sent by Mr Churchill to the Governor of Hong Kong (dated 22 February) was uncompromising. The Governor was instructed to issue a proclamation in the Colony that no compulsion of any kind would be allowed to prevent the mooi-jai from freely quitting employment. Furthermore, a Commission was to be appointed to consider legislative and administrative measures for an eventual abolition of the mooi-jai institution; to recommend proper safeguards for a system of domestic service to recommend measures to the Government to be taken in anticipation of resulting changes.[18]

In February, hotel staff and domestic servants came out in sympathetic strike with the seamen's union's strike that threatened to paralyse the Colony. The War Office felt that the strike seriously threatened Hong Kong's military security, and feared collaboration between mainland troops and Chinese strikers in Hong Kong.[19] The Joint Committee (of the Society for the Protection of Mooi-Jai and the Anti-Mooi-Jai Society) reported on 29 May.[20] Its recommendations proved unacceptable, entailing delays in the liberation of mooi-jai of up to 20 years. Also, adoption of the proposals would have implied official recognition that a system of purchasing and selling existed. To quote from the Joint Committee report: '... we realize that mui tsai keeping is a very old practice and that the interests of the owner cannot be entirely ignored, and, consequently, we are inclined to adopt the expedient of treating the purchase price of a mui tsai as money advanced to her parent. For this consideration, the mui tsai has to remain to work for her owner for a certain number of years before she regains her freedom. Only on this foundation can we hope to build up an adequate organization for effecting abolition'.

1923: The *Hong Kong Government Gazette* for 1923 announced that the Female Domestic Service Ordinance No. 1 had been passed.[21]

On 6 March the CO was informed that initial objections by Chinese members of the Legislative Council to the Ordinance had been overcome, '... that if the Government insisted on passing the measure, after they had opposed it, the labour guilds who ... were endeavouring to exploit the situation for political purposes, would claim that this was due to their support of the proposed law and that they had therefore won a victory over the representatives of the "bourgeoisie".'[22]

Then followed the clause that was to cause a great deal of trouble in the future. Governor Stubbs recommended to the CO that the introduction of a system of registration and payment of wages be deferred. Sun Yat-sen's return to Guangzhou made it necessary, according to the Governor, not to give the Chinese people cause to turn against the British administration. 'I suggest therefore that the best course will be to defer bringing Part III of the Ordinance into operation unless and until it is shown to be necessary to do so.'[23] The deferment remained widely unknown; with the passing of the Female Domestic Ordinance No. 1 public agitation ceased for a number of years.

1929: British concern centred on the perceived threat from Communists in Hong Kong and their links with Bolshevik agitators on the mainland.[24]

On 18 January the *Manchester Guardian* published a letter from John H. Harris (Anti-Slavery Society) in which he alleged that the undertaking by Mr W. Churchill in 1922 had been aborted and the public deceived as to the real situation in Hong Kong. Harris based his accusations on evidence supplied by the Anti-Mooi-Jai Society's AGM on 20 October 1928.[25] Campaigners, new and old, were galvanized into renewed action. Societies organized petitions and held assemblies.[26]

Thus the CO saw itself under considerable pressure in a politically sensitive year, the year of the General Election. Also, the lukewarm attitude of the Governor of Hong Kong, Sir C. Clementi, to the abolition of the mooi-jai system, caused embarrassment in London. The Government was firmly pledged to abolition of the system, but the Governor confined himself to promises of slight modifications of the system, dating its final disappearance at some undefined future date – granting economic improvements in China 'and a less reckless procreation of children among the poorest classes of the Chinese people.'[27] These were the objections and convictions of old, held with a firmness reminiscent of the early 1920s.

But in London the political pressures – particularly so in an election year – were different from those in Hong Kong. The electorate in Britain clamoured for action on a highly emotive issue which brought together people of all persuasions: feminists and non-feminists, liberals and radicals, reformers and conservatives, colonialists and anti-colonialists. The CO knew it was in a tight political corner: 'There are all the materials for a violent agitation of the kind we had before and every prospect of the Mui-tsai question being made a "test question" by the Feminist Societies which exploited it to the full last time. And the attack is likely to be all the more bitter on the ground that the Colonial Office and the local government have been "fooling the public" all this time. I do not like publishing the Governor's despatch if it can possibly be avoided.'[28]

In Hong Kong the Anti-Mooi-Jai Society got into gear. The Hong Kong press brought daily cases of mooi-jai, maltreated or unlawfully purchased, and daily interviews with abolitionists who criticized the official policy of deception, and the ineffectiveness of the 1923 Ordinance – all too manifest in the light sentences when a case was brought to Court.[29]

At the Anti-Mooi-Jai Society's AGM on 14 October, members advocated registration of *all* girls transferred to close a loophole that derived from the substitution of 'adopted daughter' (legal) for 'mooi-jai' (illegal).[30]

On 22 August, Lord Passfield (formerly Sydney Webb), Secretary of State for the Colonies, sent a telegram to the Governor of Hong Kong. While acknowledging his predecessor's concurrence with the delay of Part III of the 1923 Ordinance, he wrote: 'After making all allowances for the difficulties in bringing the system to an end which are described at length in your despatch, it is my duty to inform you that public opinion in this country and in the House of Commons will not accept such a result with equanimity, and that I feel myself quite unable to defend a policy of *laissez faire* in this serious matter. I must, therefore, direct that the third part of the Domestic Service Ordinance should be brought into force forthwith, and special care must be taken to inform the population generally that it is in force, and that it will not be allowed to be a dead letter. You should also at once proceed to make Regulations under Section 12 of the Ordinance for the keeping of the Registers for the remuneration of Mui Tsai and for their inspection and control.'[31]

A short time later Lord Passfield repeated in the House of Commons his intention to have the law applied in spirit as well as in letter. ' . . . I'm not prepared to aquiesce in a merely nominal enforcement of Law. Any offence against the Ordinance which comes to light should be made the subject of prosecution without regard to the position of the offender and a full Report should be furnished every six months on the working of the Ordinance, and of the proceedings taken under it.'[32]

On 8 November, the Governor of Hong Kong issued a proclamation bringing Part III of the Female Domestic Service Ordinance 1923 into force, with effect from 1 December. Regulations under paragraph 6 (2) of the Ordinance were simultaneously published, an Ordinance to Amend the Female Domestic Service Ordinance 1923.[33]

The amending Ordinance was designed to increase the efficiency of the principal Ordinance, providing for mooi-jai brought into the Colony, for the place of medical evidence in prosecution, and placed the onus of proving a girl is not a mooi-jai on the defence.

In the same year an Ordinance was passed to amend the Industrial Employment of Children Ordinance, 1922, of 1 November, an Ordinance to amend the

Protection of Women and Girls Ordinance, 1897, and the Offences Against the Person Amendment Ordinance, 1929.

1930: After initial vacillations by the Government of Hong Kong and Chinese notables about 'irksome regulations' imposed from London, followed by firm despatches from Lord Passfield, registration of mooi-jai ensued in earnest. The number registered on 1 June was given as 4,183 and declared officially to constitute all the mooi-jai living in the Colony.[34]

On 21 January, the Hong Kong press greeted the inauguration of the Society for the Prevention of Cruelty to Children which included as founder-members the most respected members of Chinese society.[35] The outgoing Governor Sir C. Clementi included in his speech, on 21 January, disparaging remarks on registration of mooi-jai which brought immediate and critical response from the CO for riding 'a high horse', for belonging to the outmoded tradition of men who assumed 'that Governors were always right and the permanent staff of the CO always wrong'.[36]

Government complacency soon came under attack as papers, such as the HKDP, and the Anti-Mooi-Jai Society expressed doubts as to whether the number of mooi-jai registered reflected the actual number of mooi-jai in Hong Kong. Newspapers also strongly criticized the Government's lack of commitment in enforcing registration.[37]

1931: The Hong Kong Society for the Protection of Children received financial support of $3,000,000; the Anti-Mooi-Jai Society received nothing.[38]

The new Governor, Sir William Peel, defined his attitude when he said that 'some' of the criticism of the mooi-jai system was perhaps well founded but that a great deal was unjustified and 'without foundation'.[39]

While on the one hand the Labour Government in London sought to make political capital out of its stance on the mooi-jai system, the CO, on the other hand, continued to be harassed by societies and individual campaigners who criticized the legislation for excluding 'adopted daughters', a term widely seen as a euphemism for mooi-jai.[40] In Hong Kong an Inspector for Mooi-Jai was appointed, assisted by two Cantonese women inspectors who were posted to the SCA in October.[41] The League of Nations questionnaire concerning trafficking in women arrived in Hong Kong.[42]

The Hong Kong Government moved to close down European brothels in the wake of the League of Nations Commission sojourn in Hong Kong.[43]

A case before the Hong Kong Magistrate concerning rape of an 'adopted daughter' threatened the edifice of mooi-jai legislation and supported the view of those in favour of registering 'adopted daughters'.[44] The defendant was freed because of insufficient evidence. He had acquired the girl in April of 1931 for $100 from her mother. The CO commented that 'if such transactions are possible in Hong Kong, then our anti-mui tsai legislation is rather a farce and the sooner something is done about "adopted daughters" the better'.[45]

1932: Controversy about adequacy of legislation continued. The District Watchmen Committee submitted its views to the debate, pleading for Government toleration and non-interference.[46]

The League of Nations Slavery Committee published its report, which remained cautiously undecided as to the nature of the mooi-jai system and considered the evidence examined inconclusive.[47] The Committee had excluded the question of procuration from its enquiry.

1933: Petitions for registration of all transferred girls continued to flood the CO.

The semi-annual report from Hong Kong on the state of the mooi-jai registration listed a high percentage as 'absconded, missing, untraceable'. (See Appendix H.) Despite CO circles' embarrassment in view of incessant public pressure, the stated policy was '. . . to avoid entering into discussion of the merits of registration of adopted daughters until we are forced to do so'.[48]

1934: In a despatch of 15 October, Sir William Peel announced the appointment of an unofficial Committee 'to consider certain proposals forwarded by the Secretary of State for the Colonies on the subject of the Mui Tsai system in Hong Kong and to report on these and kindred matters'.[49]

1935: The Committee announced the previous year published its report. Its terms of reference were so narrow that the question of the practical working of the system of registration had been excluded from its enquiry. Apart from proposing another 'full enquiry into the sale and adoption of Chinese girls' and making some minor proposals, its conclusions stressed the respectability of the mooi-jai system and its function as a preventive measure against the sale of young girls into prostitution. The CO's reaction was dissatisfaction with the inconclusiveness of the report.[50] As no evidence was taken it had become an interpretative report which reflected the conservative views of its authors.[51]

1936: On 19 February, the Secretary of State made a statement in the House of Commons on the situation of mooi-jai in Hong Kong. 'I have looked into the prosecutions and I find there are too many fines. I would like to see imprisonment as a deterrent.'[52]

The Female Domestic Service Amendment Ordinance No. 23 was passed, introducing harsher penalties for violation of law, after considerable opposition from three Chinese members of the Legislative Council and one Portuguese member, Mr Silva-Netto, who protested against the harshness of legislation.[53]

The Hong Kong Government Gazette of 8 May announced that a Mui Tsai Commission had been appointed: 'to investigate the whole question of mui tsai in Hong Kong and Malaya and any surviving practices of transferring women and children for valuable consideration, whether on marriage or adoption or in any other circumstance, and to report to the Secretary of State for the Colonies on any legislative or other action which the Commissioners may consider practicable and desirable in relation to these matters.'[54] This Commission conducted extensive interviews in Hong Kong.

1937: Publication of the Mui Tsai Commission report.[55]

While the main report advocated continuance of policies subject to minor modifications, the minority report (by Miss Picton-Turberville) suggested the need for promulgation of an Ordinance of wider scope than granted by the 1923 amended Ordinance. Instead of viewing the mooi-jai custom as suggestive of domestic servitude only, it was maintained that a much more comprehensive system of transfer was concealed by mooi-jai custom.

With the publication of this minority report public criticism of the mooi-jai legislation acquired new vigour and strong commitment emerged, especially in Britain, for its conclusions and recommendations: compulsory registration of all transferred children and periodic visitation by an approved European or Chinese female 'protector'.

The Anti-Mooi-Jai Society organized a petition to the Secretary of State for the Colonies to underline its support for legislative reforms.

1938: A third Amendment of the Female Domestic Ordinance was passed and became Ordinance No. 15. Regular inspections of the homes of registered mooi-jai were carried out until after the 1950s. By this time all girls had been declared free because of marriage or attainment of the 18th birthday when in theory no mooi-jai must be kept on by the employer-owner. With this, official recognition of the system ceased.

The Protection of Women and Girls Ordinance No. 5 was passed (as amended by No. 17 of 1946).[56] This comprehensive piece of legislation covered three fields. 'Firstly, it prohibits, with drastic penalties, any form of sexual exploitation of any woman or girl, and any attempt to harbour or detain any woman or girl for the purposes of prostitution or of emigration. Secondly, it gives the Protector (the Secretary for Chinese Affairs) extremely wide powers of investigation, if necessary by forceful entry, into any suspected case of exploitation or illegal detention of women or girls or of ill-treatment (including treatment as a drudge) of girls under twenty-one. Thirdly, it makes all adopted daughters (unless the adoption has been the subject of an order by a competent Court) automatically the statutory wards of the Protector, and makes it a criminal offence for the custodian of any such girl not to register her with the Protector. In addition the Protector may declare as his ward any other unmarried girl under the age of 21 if he has reason to believe that the girl's parent or guardian has agreed to transfer her for a valuable consideration or to part with her permanently, or has not treated her properly. Further powers are also given to the Protector to make suitable home provision for all his wards, and to carry out inspections. Between them these sections of the Ordinance extend protection to clandestine mooi-jai whom their employers might try to disguise as adopted daughters or in any other way, and also to girls who though not employed as prostitutes may reasonably be suspected of being trained or earmarked for that purpose'.[57] Sir George Maxwell commented: 'No longer will there be any question whether the child has been transferred for adoption, or quasi-adoption, whether she is a ward, a servant, a labourer under "contract", or whether she is destined to become a prostitute. As soon as the new law comes into operation and is enforced by the necessary staff of inspectors, there will be only two questions, dreadful in their simplicity and directness: at what age the girl was transferred from her parents, and whether the transfer was notified at the time to the proper authority. Unless the answers to these two questions are satisfactory, a conviction in the court will follow as a matter of course. It will be seen how this will strike at the roots of all transfers of young girls for the purpose of being trained to become prostitutes.'[58]

Accusations of slave auctions in the Colony appeared in the press, with sums, so the *Hong Kong Sunday Herald* alleged, that ranged from $50 to $250 per girl.[59] These cases of trafficking aroused much publicity. To the consternation of the CO, the Governor, Sir G. A. S. Northcote, admitted a slight increase in trafficking due to conditions of political instability in China. The CO denied any link between the mooi-jai custom, prostitution, and trafficking.[60]

Epilogue

In subsequent years the Colony saw itself faced with an ever-growing number of refugees, and with life under Japanese occupation. The mooi-jai issue vanished from the newspages.

1946: On 1 May civil government was resumed in Hong Kong. To remind the population of its duty to register adopted daughters under the 1938 Ordinance for the Protection of Women and Girls, Ordinance No. 17 was passed, stipulating compulsory registration within one month. Control of trafficking and prostitution had been in the hands of secret society leaders whose co-operation with the Japanese occupying forces had enabled them to acquire substantial areas of control. The Government had to admit difficulties in dealing with the problems of trafficking and prostitution, difficulties compounded by unrestricted immigration.[61]

1949: The total number of wards on the SCA register, on 31 March, was 853. Out of 853, 213 were listed as new registrations.[62] Staff responsible for the supervision and inspection of adopted daughters consisted of one European Inspector, who specialized in women and children's welfare work, and five Cantonese women inspectors. Miss Chan and Miss Wei had been involved in this work since 1931.[63]

1950: The Government of Hong Kong stated that, the problem of interport trafficking notwithstanding, the campaign against the mooi-jai practice had been 'reasonably' successful and official control reasserted.[64]

1956: 'No cases of Mui Tsai have come to light for a number of years and indications are that the system is discredited in the eyes of the local population.'[65]

About five months after the above telegram was sent by the Governor of Hong Kong to the Secretary of State for the Colonies, a farmer in the New Territories of Hong Kong was discovered to have kept an unregistered mooi-jai whom he had purchased for $200.[66]

Notes

1. *Hong Kong Directory & Chronicle*, 1923:965. Hong Kong.
2. *CO 129/191*. File-page: 209 24/5/1880. Dr Eitel was cited as authority for the remark.
3. Foreign Commonwealth Office. London. *Hong Kong Pamphlet*. No. 7. 'Slavery in Hong Kong'. p. 4.
4. Ibid. 17.
5. Ibid. 19.
6. IUP, *Area Studies. British Parliamentary Papers. China*. Vol. 26. op. cit.: 49–57. Correspondence respecting the Alleged Existence of Chinese Slavery in Hong Kong. HMSO. March 1882.
Dr Eitel, 'Report on the subject of domestic servitude in relation to slavery'. 25 October 1879.
7. IUP, op. cit.: 288.
8. *CO 129/231*. Despatch 46. Subject: 'Child Adoption and Domestic Services'. Report: 3. Public Records Office, Hong Kong.
9. Ibid. 5.
10. CM, 24 and 25 August 1917.
11. CM, 4 November 1919.
12. See *CO 129/466*.
13. *CO 129/463*. File page: 379.
14. 27 August 1921: 193. HKWP & . . . .
15. *CO 129/473*. Letter dated 25 May 1921.
16. Ibid. 16 February 1921.

17. *CO 129/473.*
18. Ibid.
19. *CO 129/478.* File pages: 183–6. War Office to CO. Congratulatory articles in *Canton Times*, once it became known that the CO was prepared to put pressure on Hong Kong over the mooi-jai system, added to official perturbation. Such articles were seen as inspired by Sun Yat-sen's Government, 'which is only too glad to find any handle for giving trouble to the British in Hongkong, as also to the Portuguese in Macao'. (*CO 129/478.* CO minutes. File page: 543.)
20. Despatch No. 224. *CO 129/475.*
21. 15 February 1923: 47–9.
22. Governor Stubbs to CO. *CO 129/479.* File page 535. Also, see his letter regarding the political complexion of the Chinese community in Hong Kong, dated 29 January 1930. *CO 129/483.*
23. *CO 129/479.* File pages: 440–1.
24. *CO 129/512/1* & *CO 129/512/2* for Governor's despatches on the Guangzhou situation.
25. *CO 129/514/2.* Despatch, Governor of Hong Kong to CO, 22 February.
26. The following participants, among others, were listed by the CO: Haslewoods, Col Ward, Mrs Cartwright (widow of the late editor of the HKDP), Lady and Sir J. Simon, Anti-Slavery Society, Women's Freedom League, The Association for Moral & Social Hygiene, Australian Federation of Women Voters, British Commonwealth League, Women's Non-Party Association, British Empire Union, National Union of Society for Equal Citizenship, etc., *CO 129/516.*
27. Despatch of 22 February. *CO 129/514/2.* File page: 177. Also *CO 129/514/2.* File pages: 56–64.
28. CO minutes of 10 April. *CO 129/514/2.* File pages: 16–17. The Colonial Office well knew the force of women's organizations and associations once organized behind a particular issue. The mooi-jai institution with its emotive value to propagandists could especially become a big cause in election-year.
There was a special poignancy in CO exasperation. For the first time, women had the same voting rights as men, and in the 1929 general election became a force to be reckoned with. These new voting rights meant that the number of women on the electoral register would rise to $14\frac{1}{2}$ million compared with $12\frac{1}{4}$ million men. Before the election Conservatives expressed their dismay at the prospect and they were proved right: Labour emerged for the first time as the largest single party in the House and, with Liberal's cooperation, formed the administration. 'It seemed that the prophecies that the flapper vote would lead to the downfall of the Conservative Party had come true, and Baldwin [advocate of the Bill] was much blamed.' Noreen Branson, 1976: 203, 208.
29. 17 May 1929: 676–7, 681, HKWP & ....
30. 15 October 1929, SCMP.
31. *CO 129/514/2.* File pages: 52–3.
32. 15 November 1929: 646. HKWP & ...
33. Despatch: Governor Clementi to Lord Passfield, 21 November. *CO 129/514/3.* File pages: 15–18.
34. Despatch: Hong Kong Government to Lord Passfield, 25 June 1930. Published as *Report by the Governor of Hong Kong on the Mui-Tsai Question.* December 1930. HMSO. CO. 3735. *CO 129/522/6.*
35. 24 January 1930: 116–17, HKWP & ....
36. *CO 129/524/17.* File page: 3. Sir C. Clementi was succeeded by Sir W. Peel.
37. 19 December 1930: 768, HKWP & ....

38. *CO 129/532/3*. File page: 26.
39. 25 March: 436, HKWP &....
40. *CO 129/531/4*.
41. 5 August 1932: 168, HKWP &....
42. *CO 129/533/10*.
43. *CO 129/533/10*.
44. 20 and 22 July 1931, CM.
45. *CO 129/532/5*. File page: 4.
46. *CO 129/539/4*. File pages: 118–24.
47. Report of the Committee of Experts on Slavery, Provided for by the Assembly Resolution of 25 September 1931. Slavery. League of Nations. VI.B. *Slavery. 1932. VI.B.I.* pp. 15–16.
48. *CO 129/542/10*. File page: 18.
49. *CO 129/546/9*. Despatch: 15 October 1934. HKWP &..., 13 December 1934: 789.
50. *CO 129/551/2*. File page: 68.
51. Sir George Maxwell's critique. Ibid.: 46–59.
52. 15 May 1936: 806, HKWP &....
53. 5 June 1936: 923–8, HKWP &....
54. *CO 132/78*. File page: 485.
55. *Mui Tsai in Hong Kong and Malaysia*. 1937. 2 Vols. HMSO.
56. Notified in *The Hong Kong Government Gazette*, 13 May 1938: 353–69. *CO 132/82*.
57. Based on *To the Secretary of State for the Colonies from the Officer Administering the Government*. 13 September 1950, No. 911 *Sect. File No. 3/5091/48*. Public Records Office. Hong Kong.
58. Sir G. Maxwell quoted from the 1938 Slavery Committee Report, League of Nations. Report by Sir G. Maxwell to the UN Ad Hoc Committee on Slavery. Sent by the Secretary of State for the Colonies to the Officers Administering the Government of Hong Kong, for comment. 13 December 1951. *Sec. File No. 5/5091/1948*. Public Records Office. Hong Kong.
59. *Hong Kong Sunday Herald*, 19 June 1938.
60. *CO 129/573/12*. File pages: 13–17.
61. Annual Report for Period Ending 30 June 1947. *Secretariat Files. GR 19/2706/1947*.
62. *Secretariat File. No. 1/5091/49*.
63. *Secretariat File. No. 3/5091/1948*.
64. In response to request for information on 'slavery' and related aspects from the Secretary of the UN. On 20 July 1949 the Economic and Social Council had appointed a small ad hoc Committee to survey remnants of slavery. 13 September 1950. No. 991. *Secretariat File. No. 5/5091/48*.
65. Telegram from the Governor of Hong Kong to the Secretary of State for the Colonies, 20 February 1956. *Secretariat File. File No. 3/5091/48*.
66. *South China Post Sunday Herald*. 15 July 1956.

Appendix B: Age, Designation, Price

Unless stated otherwise, reference is to girls

Year	Age	Designation	$HK Price
1918	Early teens	Unknown	70
1919	4 years	Mooi-jai	40
1920	Infant	Mooi-jai	5
1921	15 years	Concubinage	40
	Not known	Mooi-jai	55
	10 years	Resale, purpose unknown	230
1926	9 years	Mooi-jai	88
	Not known	Mooi-jai	177
1927	9 years	Mooi-jai	120
1928	Not known	Mooi-jai	5 or less
	10 years	Mooi-jai	200
1929	Boy	Adoption	250
	Not known	Mooi-jai/prostitute	80
	4 years	1st sale = mooi-jai	30
		2nd sale = ?	70
	Not known	Adopted daughter	175
	Not known	Singapore prostitute	350
	10 years	1st sale = mooi-jai	100
		2nd sale = mooi-jai	140
1930	16 years	Prostitute	100
	Teens	Mooi-jai	110
	10 years	Mooi-jai	120
	10 years	Mooi-jai	145
		⎧ Mooi-jai resold into Singapore brothel	440
	Not known	⎨ Mooi-jai resold	200
		⎩ Mooi-jai resold into Hong Kong brothel	350
	Young woman	Concubinage	200
	11 years	Mooi-jai	150
1931	Teens	Mooi-jai	130
	3 years	Mooi-jai	39
1932	Not known	To pay debt	70
	13 years	Mooi-jai	100
	Not known	Mooi-jai	120
	14 years	Adopted daughter	120
	13 years	Adopted daughter	70
		⎧ Mooi-jai	110
	Not known	⎨ Mooi-jai	144
		⎩ Mooi-jai	125
	Young widow	Prostitute	130
	Young widow	Prostitute	90
		⎧ Mooi-jai	170
	Not known	⎨ Mooi-jai	100
		⎨ Mooi-jai	100
		⎩ Mooi-jai	100

	13 years	Mooi-jai	100
1933	7 years	Mooi-jai	130
	7 years	Mooi-jai	100
	13 years	1st sale = mooi-jai	100
		2nd sale = mooi-jai	140
1934	Not known	{Pledge for loan	160
		{Pledge for loan	100
1935	2 year old boy	Adoption	85
1936	3 weeks/boy	Adoption	35
	6 year old boy	Adoption	100
	15 years	Mooi-jai, pledge for loan	100
	5 days	27	
	Not known	Adopted daughter	200
	7 year old boy	Adoption	65
	Not known	Mooi-jai	120
1938	8 years	Adopted daughter	75
	5 years	Adopted daughter	15
	16 years	Macau prostitute	150
	5 years		19
1940	Under 10 years		16

I have accepted 'adopted daughter' for the column designation, although in many cases it was but a euphemism for mooi-jai.

Appendix C: Deed of Sale (South China, 1927)

This deed of sale is made by Poon Shi of Mak family.

In consequence of urgent need for funds to meet family expenses, I am willing to sell my own daughter, Ah Mui, 10 years of age, born in the afternoon, 23rd day of 11th moon, Mo Ng year (i.e. 25th December, 1918), to Chan Yee Koo through a go-between. In the presence of three parties, it is mutually agreed and arranged that the purchase price is to be 141 dollars. After this sale, Chan Yee Koo shall have the right to change the name of the girl. If the girl is disobedient, Chan Yee Koo shall be allowed to resell her, and the mother shall have no recourse. In the event of any misfortune befallen the girl, there is no blame to either Party.

It is also made perfectly clear that the girl has never been betrothed to any other family, nor is there any mortgage on her. In case any question arises as to the origin of the girl, the seller Poon Shi of Mak Family is held responsible, and it in no way concerns the buyer.

This is a straightforward sale and purchase between two parties and lest verbal contract is invalid, delivered to Chan Yee Koo as proof thereof.

Poon Shi of Mak Family hereby acknowledges receipt of the purchase price of 141 dollars in full, without deduction.

Finger prints of Poon Shi of Mak Family...
Go-between, Poon Shi of Chan Family.

Dated

The Republic of China, 13th June, 1927.

The original, which is now in the Anti-Slavery Society Archive (Rhodes Library, Oxford), was sent by the Anti-Mooi-Jai Society Secretary, J. D. Bush, to Mrs Haslewood (the British Anti-Mooi-Jai compaigner) who handed it over to the M.P., Sir John Simon (husband of the author of *Slavery*, Lady Simon). Sir John read out the deed in the House of Commons, creating a considerable stir.

Appendix D: Deed of Sale (Guangzhou, about 1895)

The makers of this deed for the absolute sale of a girl for the purpose of prostitution are the Tang family, who had a girl for prostitution surnamed... and named... aged 16. She was born at the Nai Watch on the 6th day of the 10th moon Kang Shon year. They wished to sell her to anyone, no matter he lived near them or at a distance, or whether he lived on land or afloat. The price demanded was 270 dollars. Through go-between Li Shi, the girl was taken to... who examined her and found her all right, and agreed to pay the amount demanded, viz. 270 dollars, at the rate of 71 to the dollar. Matters were explained in the presence of the three parties, and the two parties mutually agreed to the bargain. A deed was drawn up for the transaction this day in the presence of the go-between, and both the girl and the deed and the full price were handed over and all matters concluded. This girl has never been betrothed to any family. Whenever the sale is complete the girl is to go away for ever. No enquiries will ever be made after her nor will anyone come to see her or visit her. The purchaser has a right to have the girl taught to play music and taught singing in order that she might be put on the river as a prostitute, and she will dress herself up to receive visitors as her calling and to thus spend her life. There shall be nothing said to the contrary. The sale was an open sale and the purchase was an open purchase; there was no implication of any kidnapping nor was there any compulsory act. It was neither a set off against debts nor a matter of the like nature. She is not a malformed girl, she is free from leprosy, and has not suffered from fits, and if she is found to be suffering from any of these diseases the vendor is willing to return all the money to the purchaser. Should any death or accidents befall her each party will abide by the will of heaven. Should any question arise in future as to where the girl was got from, it will be the business of the vendor and the go-between to settle such a question. Last words of mouth should not be evidence; this deed for the absolute sale of the girl for the purposes of prostitution is made to be handed over and kept as proof. The Tang family received 270 dollars in full at 71 to the dollar as purchase money for the girl sold for the purposes of prostitution. Nothing is left owing.

HKWP &... 4 July 1895: 11.

The document was authenticated by fingermarks. This sung-tip became public knowledge in a case at the Hong Kong Supreme Court, on 27 June 1895, involving a charge of enticing a girl to Hong Kong for the purposes of prostitution.

Appendix E: Deed of Sale (South China, about 1910)

We the mediators of [this] perpetual deed for the absolute sale of a niece [the daughter of sister-in-law] are Chan A Ping [her] maternal uncle and Lau Shi his [Chan A Ping's] wife, native of Tsang Shing district, and Li Lin T'ai, the girl's elder sister. On account of urgent necessities [Li Lin T'ai] was willing to let her younger sister named Li Kin T'ai, born at the Ts'au hour on the 26th day of the 2nd moon of the Ki Hoi year be first [offered for sale] to clansmen and others alike; but none of them would like to buy her. Then by the introduction of mediators – Tsang A Hau and Shui A Kwai – of the Ip Tak Wo T'ong, it is agreed by them to accept the sale [of the girl] as a servant. It is distinctly agreed that the consideration price is 126 dollars, each at the weight of 7 [mace] 1 [candareen]. It is expressly agreed to in the presence of three parties and with the consent of both sides. The transaction has this day been completed in the presence of all parties. The deed and [consideration] money have been mutually handed over without leaving anything owing. After the sale the buyer shall be at liberty to alter her name for service, and when she is grown up to open negotiation for her marriage. Should there be any doubt as to her antecedents the vendors and the mediators shall have to clear it, and the purchaser is not to be concerned [in the matter]. Either party must regard all mishap or kidnapping, if any, as the will of heaven. After purchasing this is not a case of kidnapping, fraud, compulsion, or in satisfaction of a debt, etc. Lest words of mouth should bear no evidence, this deed of sale is clearly made and handed over to the Ip Tak Wo T'ong* to be kept as proof.

Really received by the hands of Chan A Ping and his wife Lau Shi the sum of 126 dollars, each at the weight of 7 [mace] 1 [candareen] being the consideration money for sale of the girl.

Mediators Tsang A Hau	(finger mark)
Shui A Kwai	"

The person making this deed for the sale of the girl

Chan A Ping	(own pen)
Lau Shi	(finger mark)

Sung Tung third year intercalary, 6th moon, 50th day.

HKDP 19 October 1911: 12.
Published in full translation. Read out in the course of the hearing of a kidnapping case at the Supreme Court on 18 October 1911.

* I suspect that the Ip Tak Wo T'ong must have been the lineage hall where the transaction took place and the sung-tip was lodged.

Appendix F: Note of Presentation (South China, 1924)

This Presentation Note was made by Au Yeung Sheung and his wife, Chan Shi. Not being able to take care of their own daughter owing to high cost of living, they are willing to present her to someone. At first their relatives were asked to take her but none would or could do so. Then, Au Yeung Ling, a go-between, introduced her to Chung Ying Liu, who agreed to adopt her as a fostered daughter, and further agreed to reimburse to the parents of the girl a sum of 95 dollars being cost of ginger and vinegar (maintenance expenses). It was arranged and agreed by the three parties, and full payment of the sum of 95 dollars was made on this day to deliver the child to Chung Ying Liu.

After the child has been handed over to the Chung family Chung Ying Liu will take good care of her, and when she comes of age, she will be married by order of

Chung Ying Liu and at the same time her parents will be informed of her marriage so that they may have the right to visit thereafter.

In case of any misfortune befalling the girl, it is Heaven's decree.

Lest words of mouth should not be sufficient, this Presentation Note is given to Chung Ying Liu as proof.

The girl was born in Ding Shi year, 9th moon, 'Chi' time [about 10 a.m.] a native of Pak Tang Kong Me, in Shun Tak district [14/11/17].

Au Yeung Sheung and wife hereby acknowledge receipt of the sum of 95 dollars.

Au Yeung Sheung	(signed)
Chan Shi	(finger print)
Au Yeung Ling – Go-between	(finger print)

Republic of China, 13th year, 10th Moon, 28th day, i.e. 24/11/24.

A copy of this Presentation Note is lodged at the Anti-Slavery Society Archive, File: G 691 (Rhodes Library, Oxford).

Appendix G: Committee of the Anti-Mooi-Jai Society: 1928

The Committee embraced in all 39 members, six of whom were women. Two worked at the YWCA, which had always shown great interest in the mooi-jai issue. One woman was associated with a Company, one woman had the profession of a priest. Unlike women of the upper-class these women had ties with organisations or groupings outside kinship and therefore some experience with occupying positions in the public world.

Two Europeans belonged to the Committee, one of them was married to a Chinese woman.

Twenty-six Chinese men had their professions listed: 4 merchants, 1 compradore, 4 clerks, 5 teachers, 5 priests, 3 doctors, 1 dentist, 1 bank-manager, 2 journalists. The composition of the Committee was thus solidly middle-class.

(WA TSZ YAT PO, 23 October 1928. Quoted in *CO 129/514/2*. File pages: 181–2).

Appendix H: Official Statistics of the Progress of the Mooi-Jai Campaign in Hong Kong 1930–37

	Dec. 1930	June 1931	Jan. 1932	June 1932	Jan. 1933
Total No.	(July '29)	(Nov. '30)	(May '31)	(Nov. '31)	(May '32)
Registered	4,299 a	4,117	3,949	3,741	3,482
Diminution:					
Returned to parents	53	34	82	83	55
Married	48	60	59	78	56
Disappeared	31	29 b	21 c	26 d	29
Left colony	29	24 e	29	116	83
Obtained employment elsewhere	13	12	10	19	26
Died	5	3	3	5	5
In charge of SCA	2	6	4	1	1 (reg. 4 cancelled)
Wrongly registered	1				
Total:	182	168	208	328	259
Total no. registered	Nov. '30 4,117	May '31 3,949	Nov. '31 3,741	May '32 3,482	Nov. '32 3,017

Source: Half-yearly reports by the Governor of Hong Kong, on progress of the Mooi-jai campaign, to League of Nations; *Slavery*, League of Nations: 1935: 45–58.

	July 1933	Dec. 1933	June 1934	Nov. 1934	May 1935
Total No.	(Nov. '32)	(May '33)	(Nov. '33)	(June '34)	(Nov. '34)
Registered	3,017	2,820	2,749	2,508	2,291
Diminution:					
Returned to parents	44	56	47	43	49
Married	43	34	43	32	39
Disappeared	29	22	12	16	12
Left colony	72	86	85	54	27
Obtained employment elsewhere	24 f	25 g	56 h	39 i	34 j
Died	9	5	2	3	1
In charge of SCA	(3 sent to Po Leung Kuk)	(1 sent to to French Convent)			
	9	10	6	10	6
Wrongly registered			(remains with family, status of kin)	(removed from reg.)	(conv. of larceny)
		1	1	20	1
Total:	233	241	243	217	169
Total no. registered	(May '33)	(Nov. '33)	(May '34)	(Nov. '34)	(May '35)
	2,820 k	2,749	2,504	2,291 l	2,122 m

Source: League of Nations, *Slavery*, 1935: 45–58; 1936: 43–6.

	Nov. 1935	May 1936	Nov. 1936	May 1937
Total no. registered	(May '35) 2,122	(Nov. '35) 1,952	(May '36) 1,723	(Nov. '36) 1,599
Diminution:				
Returned to parents	40	42	33	30
Married	34	82	21	30
Disappeared	12	5	6	6
Left colony				
Obtained employment elsewhere	32	55 (3 removed from reg.)	31	15
	35	31	16	13
Died	2	3		3
In charge of SCA	15	10	13	
Wrongly registered		(conv. of larceny)	(removed from reg.)	(removed from reg.)
		1	4	13
Total	170	299	124	125
Total no. registered	(Nov. '35) 1,952[n]	(May '36) 1,723[o]	(Nov. '36) 1,599[p]	(May '37) 1,474[q]

Source: League of Nations, *Slavery*, 1936: 67–70; 1937: 21; 1938: 19–22, 27–31.

Notes:

a. A subsequent correction stated the original number of mooi-jai to have totalled 4,368. By January 1932 total diminution amounted to 558.

b. In all 33 had disappeared, eventually 4 were found.

c. Out of 22 who had disappeared, one was found.

d. 1 was removed to an unknown address.

e. 25 had left the colony, 1 returned eventually.

f. 19 entered domestic service.

g. 19 entered domestic service.

h. 43 entered domestic service.

i. 28 entered domestic service.

j. 25 entered domestic service.

k. 36 were traced from the statistics that appeared in the January report of 1933; the net decrease thus only amounted to 197, as they had already been accounted for in the total diminution of 259.

l. Under 15 years, 975; 15–18 years, 1,031; over 18 years, 285; total registered 2,291.

m. Age-groups: under 15 years, 719; 15–18 years, 987; over 18 years, 416; total registered 2,122.

n. Prosecutions (Dec. 1929 – June 1934): Charges of cruelty, 30; keeping unreg. mooi-jai, 113; failing to pay adequate wages, 12.
(June 1934 – May 1935): charges of cruelty, 7; keeping unreg. mooi-jai, 49; failing to pay adequate wages, 2; failing to notify changes in address, in status of mooi-jai, etc., 39.

(May 1935 – November 1935): charges of cruelty, 6; keeping unreg. mooi-jai, 45; failing to pay adequate wages, 2; failure to notify changes in circumstances of mooi-jai, 45.

o. In 1936 hitherto unregistered mooi-jai were discovered. Accessibility to supervision for registered mooi-jai was as follows:

	Total on register	Missing
visited regularly by inspectors	1,489	732
living on boats	94	54
in the New Territories	140	25
	1,723	811

Mooi-jai age-groups: under 15 years, 456; 15–18 years, 791; over 18 years, 476; total, 1,723.

p. Out of a total of 1,599 registered mooi-jai 807 were reported missing. 50 prosecutions were made, including 4 charges of cruelty.

Mooi-jai age-groups: under 15 years, 432; 15–18 years, 727; 19–31 years, 440; total, 1,599.

q. Out of a total of 1,474 registered mooi-jai, 790 were reported as missing. 29 prosecutions included 2 charges of cruelty.

Mooi-jai age groups: under 15 years, 306; 15–18 years, 601; 19–32 years, 567; total, 1,474.

The SCA employed Inspector Fraser and two Chinese female assistants to supervise registered mooi-jai and inspect cases of abuse and law evasion.

Index